to a kn
lovniy kany
so much love

Anis

YOU ARE THE ONE

YOU ARE THE ONE

AVIS BAUM

Cover image: Fermi Epicycles: The Vela Pulsar's Path
Credit: NASA, DOE, International Fermi LAT Collaboration
Design: Scott Bricher

Dedicated to the One I love

Contents

AUTHOR'S NOTE

Just a quick note before we begin.

This book is a journey, and like any adventurous journey, its intent is to move you out of your outward reality and into your inward reality. As such, it does not conform to this outer world's common conventions, and therefore you will find unusual punctuation, capitalization, repetition of concepts, and other methods of catching you off guard, of moving you out of your comfort zone, just enough to explore a different Way.

The journey inward is what unlocks the key to Life, revealing no less than our reason for Being.

CHAPTER 1

THE KINGDOM OF HEAVEN IS WITHIN
SPIRITUALITY: IT'S AN INSIDE JOB

"A miracle is nothing more or less than this.
Anyone who has come into a knowledge
of his true identity, of his oneness with the
all-pervading wisdom and power, has made
it possible for higher laws than the ordinary
mind knows to be revealed to him."
Ralph Waldo Trine

Everything you will hear, see, and feel in this book you already recognize and know to be true.

If there is anything you do not resonate with or find to be untrue, then perhaps you are not in full remembrance of it yet, or it is still a construct of my ego trying to slip in, and for this I do apologize ahead of time.

I will ask you a favor, though: Please suspend disbelief. Read this as you would a novel, allowing your mind to fall asleep and your heart to awaken. Think of it as an adventure in which you are the main character. Go without judgments, without analysis, just be present, just hold love in your heart, and most of all enjoy! Allow yourself to think outside the box, for as we move forward on our journey of self discovery we discover that *there is no box.* Life is but an illusion that is in place to serve us.

Why am I writing this book?

I write to offer a few things I know to be true. I know that spiritual truths are simple, and I know that these truths resonate with us, if we can still ourselves long enough to listen to our Inner Voice. I know that these truths live inside of us. I know we have become so hurried, dense, outwardly motivated and individualized that we have forgotten who we are, who's the boss, why we are here,and where we are going.

We need to retrieve that which is within, that which is innate, that which is our birthright. We need to retrieve our inner compass and find our way Home, and the way we do that is by REMEMBERING and going WITHIN. It is about REMEMBRANCE— that we are in this together and that we are here to remind each other of who we are and why we are here…that we are all ONE and that we are all spirit in human form. We have forgotten this, that we are part of the One, the One that created us.

So here it is. I hope this book and its words help you, as they have helped me, on my journey of self discovery, to remember and discover who I truly am, and that you and I, WE, ARE NOT SEPARATE BUT WE ARE ONE all united by a Divine spark within us.

There is but only One of us here.

Mystical messages , magical timing

I believe that the universe provides us with exactly what we need at exactly the right time, so: If you are reading this book at this time, there is something for you inside. Take what you need from it, and discard the rest. Some of what is in here may be too far out there, too outside the box for you. That's ok, but make sure to maybe take a look again in a few months!

I know that, for me, books are magical, and especially books on spirituality. They seem to give me exactly what I need to hear at just the right time. But there is an interesting phenomenon that happens to me when I reread some of my spiritual books: Months later there are new insights in them that I missed the first time. It is as if the book is now magically providing me what I need to hear, exactly at the right point in my spiritual development, or it's offering a new insight that I wasn't quite ready to hear at an earlier time.

So spirituality is an inside job. But what does this mean, and exactly how do we bring it Home to our lives?

First, everyone's path is right, good, and valid, no matter what the outside appearance is. So wherever you are, wherever you are coming from, and wherever you have been your path has been perfect and you are perfect .What we will explore and journey into in this book is an opportunity to begin peeling away the layers, masks, and constructs that are keeping us from being our AUTHENTIC SELF.

To do this we remember simple truths and tools that have been given to all of us. We still have them, they are just hidden inside of us, and sometimes we just need to quiet down to hear them, i.e.: become blind to see. What I mean about becoming blind in order to have Eyes to See is that we need to go within and see with our Inner Eyes. If we are looking outside of ourselves for fulfillment, we will never find it, and we will never See.

Become a blind seer

In meditation, I close my outside eyes and become blind, in order to activate my Inner Sight and SEE. As we progress through this book, we begin to understand that everything we need is within us, that this is a truth. There's a great saying that I love, "if you don't go within you will go without. " This has many layers of meaning, depending on where you stand on your journey, but it will apply to almost everything in this book, as it applies to everything in my life.

We can wander the world aimlessly and endlessly, looking for happiness, love, light, fulfillment, joy, lightness of being, abundance, gratitude, kindness, ecstasy, and bliss, and the only place we will ever truly find it, where it is permanent and eternal, is WITHIN ourselves. We find it in ourselves first and become whole, unified, and then we find this love reflected in our outside world.

"Spirituality happens when you receive the call to go in, " says Michael Beckwith. "The kingdom of heaven is within you." It is our inward journey of self that leads us to Heaven. It is an inside job. The world provides us with exactly what we need to begin our journey Home, and then the universe gives us more signs and points us in the right direction. It's when we finally reach a point where we have done all the right things, or all the wrong things, and we are still not fulfilled, that we begin our inner exploration, and it is here where we eventually find what we are looking for. We begin to discover who we are, why we are here, and eventually on this path we find our compass, reclaim our spirit, our Divinity, and our Wholeness.

My work as a healer and an intuitive has been to help people discover who they are, to help them find their voice, their compass, and to help them live an authentic life. It is a most beautiful journey to share with someone, so replete with love and adventure. It never ceases to amaze me when someone comes to the realization that their purpose wasn't really to be a mom, a dad, a plumber, a banker etc - these were just pieces of the puzzle, leading them to where they needed to go, but their true purpose is to "BECOME ONE" again, to be free again from the illusion, to find "HEAVEN ON EARTH" right here, right now.

When the pirates took us over

A long, long time ago we lived in paradise. We were co-creators with spirit, individualized but whole and One. WE were united, not separate. We were able to create and manifest at will, and as soon as a thought was thought, it appeared in manifest form. Everything we created served the whole, and everyone within the whole, as we lived in total cooperation and harmony. We drank and fed from the tree of life and we created such beauty and an incredible way to live and Be. Everyone's needs were met and taken care of; we all had purpose, and we were immortal. Then we began to notice that some began to create for themselves separately from the whole, and for their own benefit. Separation occurred. We began the rift of mind and heart—or spirit—and we became separate. We became divided and started to focus on how we were separate and different. We disconnected from each other. We became greedy and self motivated, we lost the captain of our ship.

We lost our compass, and the pirates took over.

We drank from the tree of knowledge, instead of the tree of life. The tree of knowledge was all about this world and its duality and fear, worry, hatred, separation, disease, war, and death. We became denser, and denser still, until we completely forgot who we truly are. We then began an endless cycle of reincarnation. Linear time and space began, and this is where we are in the illusion now.

That was our outward journey from spirit, and I believe many of us are on our inward journey back to source, back to the tree of life, back to wholeness and back to paradise. Back to Heaven on Earth. We are waking up from the dream of separation, for it is but a dream that we have made real. It is an illusion that we are separate, and all we need to get back there, to the place we really never left, is to REMEMBER, to regain the captain of our own ship and journey Home.

If you wish to go there, then all you need to do is do the WORK. The work is to "Know thyself," discover who you are, find Spirit within and become whole again.

CHAPTER 2

✳

KNOW THYSELF

I have a beautiful friend named Whitney who has started a foundation in Africa, helping children with AIDS. She is an amazing light worker, aiding children on every level, mental, emotional, physical, and spiritual. She has called a couple of times when she has needed help, specifically with two children who were hours away from death. Both children are alive and well today. She is an angelic presence on this plane. This time Whitney called on behalf of herself, for as light workers we need support, too.

The message came through that she must take care of herself first, if she is going to help others; that she needed to get away immediately for a couple of days somewhere near the water, to recuperate and restore, and that she would know where to go. She was also told that she would be finding crystals there. I told her to get off the phone, begin meditating, and I was told that the healing work on her would start immediately.

Whitney called me after she came back from her trip and relayed what had happened. She said that as soon as we hung up she felt this incredible weight lifted out from her field, and a beautiful white light replaced it and engulfed her. After that she got on the computer and started to look for places in South Africa where she could go that were near water. She had a list of about fifteen places and she knew immediately, from looking at the list, which one she should pick and enjoy.

She left the next day for her trip. She said that the whole time she was there she felt like the place had been cleared of people and only those she was to meet remained. All the other "normal" visitors seemed to have been cleared, and there was a magical sense and vibrancy to the place, almost so magical that it seemed as if it might disappear after she left. As soon as she had arrived at the destination and approached the water, a woman started walking toward her, and they began to speak. The woman explained that she was a healer who used crystals in her practice, but that she was stopping her work and had been told that someone would be coming *at this time to receive some of her crystals. Whitney told her that she had been guided there herself and been told she would find crystals there. I am lucky enough to own one of those crystals that Whitney brought back for me.*

How do we figure out who we are and why we are here?

It is truly so, *so simple*, and it is also truly so, so difficult, a journey that requires incredible strength and courage. As you read this, you might even think, *This is just too easy and it simply cannot work.* But spiritual truths and tools *are* simple, though as humans we may find them hard to follow, we lose our discipline, we slip, we get lost. Eventually, though, we discover who we are, and that's when we learn that we are all Divine, we are all Love, we are all sparks of Mother/Father God, and that we are all created equal in this way, united in this field as One.

Following are some of the simple tools I have found to be helpful as we travel our way Home.

The illness that brought me to the silence

MEDITATION: BECOMING BLIND IN ORDER TO SEE. Later I will discuss how I believe we put certain obstacles in our life path in order to help us evolve and learn the lessons that lead us HOME. One such lesson came into my life in the form of illness that looked to be a "bad" thing, but this "bad" thing forced me to become still, to find myself within.

I have come to understand over time that we live in a benevolent world that gives us exactly what we need in order to evolve, so I no longer think of things as "good" or "bad." I just see that if they are in my life, they are there for a reason and that reason in the end is a good one, even if it may feel "painful" or "bad."

Here's how and why I began meditating. I had been diagnosed with babesia, erlichiosis, and Lyme disease all at once. The Lyme disease had settled in my brain and my brain was riddled with lesions. The other diseases were affecting my blood; all of them impaired my immune system and my ability to heal. My very Western but enlightened doctor advised me to seek the help of holistic remedies and alternative therapies in order to heal. What I did not realize at the time was that my healing had to come on many levels: physical, emotional, and spiritual, and of course they were all linked.

I began by meditating half an hour a day, every day, with meditation audiotapes. I spent many a morning in a pool of tears, begging for healing, and only connecting to stillness. I began to realize that, even though it seemed like a waste of time, and that I was doing "nothing," on the days I meditated I felt more peaceful and, even though I was still in a lot of physical pain, I felt better emotionally and spiritually.

Eventually I surrendered to the process and meditated diligently, nonstop, every day without exception, for six months. Then, one day in the quiet and the stillness, in the darkness behind my closed eyes, a very small light appeared. Then the light turned into a window, and suddenly everything was filled with light.

What I was told in Spirit

On that day I knew who I was and why I am here.

I had connected to my guides, my ascended masters, to Source and to my life purpose. I was told I would become a healer, that I would assist people with their life journey, and that I would help people on their path of self-discovery, through their ascension and on their way Home.

I had accessed my inner sight. Without the trials of disease, which we generally consider to be "bad," I would not have taken the time to meditate or to go inward, to gradually discover that everything on this plane is "Love"- that there is no good or bad. Instead, I saw that it all serves us, that it is all of the Light, that this world is only an illusion, helping us, guiding us Home.

What is meditation? It is about quieting down, becoming still and present at the same time. This can take the form of traditional meditation or it can be a walk in nature, looking at the sunset, dancing, and so on. But in the end meditation is being present with yourself, and it can be our state all the time, depending on our level of practice. Why should we ever disconnect from our meditative state? From our connection to self?

I know Einstein found that the state between being awake and being asleep is where he found his answers. He also had a hard time staying in the in-between place without falling completely into the dream state, so he would sit in a chair holding a ball in his hand, so that if he drifted into sleep the ball would fall and it would be just enough to wake him up slightly, just enough to allow him to stay in the in-between place where he found his answers to the questions of the world.

Steven Spielberg finds a lot of his ideas while driving. I do not recommend this, as it could be dangerous, but it works for him. Find the place for you, so you can expand this magical state into every part of your life. Discover who you are. "IT'S ALL INSIDE." I think J C Penney got it right with their slogan.

Pieces of the divine puzzle, that's us

KNOW THYSELF: The journey of the SELF is the journey into SPIRIT. You have to do the WORK. It is the great WORK. The work begins when we start peeling away the layers that keep us from being our AUTHENTIC selves. As we discover who we are, we are re-introduced to our Spirit, learning that we are DIVINE and we are all ONE. We are all like puzzle pieces, all Divine, perfect, and distinct. Find what puzzle piece you are, be that, and once you do that you connect to the other complete puzzle pieces to become ONE. All puzzle pieces are part of the Whole. Every puzzle piece is as important as every other piece, even if each one is different. I always think it so funny that when we come into this world each of us is unique… and then we all try to be the same, becoming opaque along the way.

Then we see someone vibrant and authentic and we want to be like them, but this does not work. Do not mirror people. Instead, find out who *you* are, what makes *you* vibrant and beautiful. I love the way people who are comfortable in their skin radiate a sense of life, breath, and beauty, *bien dans sa peau.* Comfortable in their own skin, so to speak. If you want to be and feel like them, BE YOU. Take the time to rediscover who you are. Take all the layers off that you put on as protection, that you thought would allow you to fit in, and find your compass, get to know yourself again. Use healers, therapists, stillness, and friends to assist you. Do whatever it is you need to do to get you there.

QUIET THE MIND: It took me two years to quiet my mind. First I had to figure out the voice I was hearing in my head. *Is that voice me? Does it speak for me? Does it have a mind of its own? Does it serve my higher or lower self? What is it telling me?* That voice had been with me so long, I thought it was me and that I had no power over it, that I was meant to just listen endlessly to its idle chatter and negative messages.

We began in the Unified Field

I began to read a book around that time called *The Voice of Knowledge: A Practical Guide to Inner Peace,* by Janet Mills and Don Miguel Ruiz, the author of T*he Four Agreements.*

This is an invaluable book to read if you are ready to find peace and still your mind. It says that basically we came into this world as innocents, with a deep understanding that comes from the heart, a Unified Field where we are all One. We grow up in this world and begin to separate, as we realize that the world functions in duality and separation, that there has been a change of state from the place we came from, which was Unity. As we grow, our parents, teachers, and family start showing us the way to be in this land, and how it works, and we quickly begin to realize that if we are going to be accepted and loved we'd better adapt the beliefs of our family, our teachers, our tribe, and our nation or we will be left out in the cold, unloved and alone.

So we begin to buy into things that our heart just knows are not right for us, such as the belief that our group of people is better than that group of people, or that men are superior to women. We see this duality often in the most spiritual-seeming places, such as religions, where we are taught that our religion will get you to heaven, while others won't. That men can hold spirit and be such representatives of spirit as ministers, priests, or rabbis, while women can't. That gay people can't expect the same rights as the rest of us.

"We are not equal" is always the message. We are "superior," "better."

But at the same time there is a little voice in our head, sometimes accompanied by a contraction in our gut, telling us that what we are hearing and seeing just doesn't sound right, and it certainly doesn't feel right. In spite of that voice, that tug, however, we disregard our inner compass and take on the beliefs of our group, for we want to fit in, follow and be loved. We tell our inner voice to shut up as we put on our masks, moving further away from our authentic selves. We are doing what others want us to do in order to survive.

Our half-life behind the mask

Eventually we have put on so many masks in order to fit in and be loved that we don't even remember who we are, what we truly believe. We are like walking zombies, asleep to who we are. One of the side effects of all this is that our mind goes crazy, as if it has a virus. We did not listen, so now our mind has a mind of its own and it is bossing us around, talking to us non-stop, filling us with negative thoughts and keeping us captive in this zombie-like state

Our ego, our separated part, does not want us to wake up, for it fears annihilation. Unlike so many, I don't believe that either our ego or our mind is our enemy, by the way. Like everything else, they are here to help us and teach us. One way the mind ultimately supports us is to drive us so crazy with its negative chatter that we finally have to do something about it, becoming so miserable that we start looking for answers. Here's where we can start our process of self-discovery and our inward journey to Wholeness. This is where we start questioning the autocrat in our head. We begin to realize that, if we are looking at these thoughts, and having separate thoughts about the thoughts, we must be more than just the chatter in our head. For who is the person watching and thinking about what the thoughts are saying? It has to be someone else other than the voice in my mind.

Eckhart Tolle describes this realization perfectly in his book, *A New Earth*.

When I was at this stage in my journey, I realized my mind could offer compassion, empathy, and acceptance toward others and toward my friends. They could be upside down, screwing up royally, and I could forgive them and love them. That was not the problem; the problem was that I could not extend this same kindness to myself. Anything I did was under 24/7 scrutiny. Nothing I did could be good enough. No, I could have, should have, done it more, less, better, bigger, smaller.

Eventually I bottomed out on that and made a deal with the voice in my head.... *You must give me the same kindness and respect you give others, otherwise I will not listen.* Slowly my ultimatum began to work, except in times of crisis, when the voice would still be relentless. In those times I had to override it with a chant, "I am love, I am light, I am love, I am light, I am love, I am light." Eventually the voice would become still, and I would find Peace.

Today this voice and I are unified and working together. It rarely goes out of balance or back into the negativity and mindless chatter. When that does happen, I simply thank it, and ask, *Ok, when was it that I was not my authentic self? Where did I let someone pierce my boundary so that I would lose my voice? Where did I not stand up to my principles? Where am I so out of integrity that you, the voice, need to call me on it?*

I go back, find the place, find my voice, make amends, say sorry where and if appropriate, and move forward in Peace. It seems to me that we have all developed a virus in our heads, and we must remove it first, erase it, quiet it down, and then reboot it in Unity. We will speak more later about how this ties in with WHO"S THE BOSS? Who is really in charge and who are we at our core? Stilling the mind is a key component of our journey back to the self, to the remembrance of who we are.

Asking and giving permission

ASK AND YOU SHALL RECEIVE: There are many practices I do that keep me balanced, and one of them is to ask for what I am needing in my life at the moment. I believe that we can access an abundant energy that is ready to assist us in any way possible, but that this energy needs our permission, as there is free will, in order to assist us. I truly believe that when we ask, we are always answered. The answer may not look the way we thought it would, but we must be ready to accept the answer; we must trust it, knowing it is exactly what we need and that it is offering us what we require in order to get to a better place. Sometimes it may show up as something that looks like a setback, but is actually an opportunity to make a different choice, maybe to change jobs, perhaps we even got fired, or we have to move, or the like.

It is only when we look back that we see how this setback actually served us, and how it truly was the answer to our prayers. So why stress? Know that everything in your life is there to help you and try to release the emotional components of it that are holding you in pain, suffering, fear, and worry.

We are Spirit in human bodies and we are here to evolve as Spiritual Beings. Earth is the school we do this in, and it is transitory. Once we leave these bodies we are still Spirit. Choose now to see this, and you will be enlightened. *Be in this world but not of it.* Embrace who you are. The lessons that come your way are not there to hurt you, but to help you, some placed by the universe, some you personally put onto your path when you were setting up your life plan before you incarnated into this life. *You* chose where to incarnate, who your parents would be, your religion, if any. You chose the perfect circumstances that you thought would provide the environment and lessons necessary in order to evolve spiritually.

SELF-MATTERS: When we began to put masks around us and began acting in the way we thought would please others in order so that we could fit in, be accepted and loved, we began to lose ourselves. This is a universal journey. We have all done it, we all go through it, but we are all not conscious of it.

When we live in relationship, and most of us do, we

often act and do things for others instead of doing things for ourselves, and by guessing and acting in the way we think the others would like, we become inauthentic. *Acting* is the key word. Not being ourselves. The problem is that the person doing this, even if they are loved and accepted, retains a piece of themselves deep inside that is saying... *Wow, if they truly knew who I am, and if I acted the way I truly prefer and showed myself fully, shadow and all, they would hate me. I would not be loved.*

This is a Catch 22, for even if they seem to feel love, they still feel unloved, or not truly loved, as they feel the mask is being loved, not them, and that the love is conditional. *I will love you if you behave this way or that way, if not I will not love you.* The other problem with this whole issue is that we become experts at reading people and giving them what they want, so much so that we begin to forget what we want, what makes us tick, and we lose our way and our compass.

Being lost can be a good thing

I cannot tell you how many people come into my practice with no idea who they are anymore. They do not know who they are, what their likes and dislikes are. They are completely lost. If you are in this place, do not despair, this is a really good sign, you are at the

point of a big breakthrough. They—and perhaps you—
have done all the "right things" society and family have
taught them, they have sacrificed themselves entirely
and given all their love to others. They show up at my
office because they are sick, their marriages are not
working, their children have no boundaries, and everything is out of control. Their life from the outside looks
perfect and harmonious, but to those living in it there
is a malaise that permeates everything. I find women
seem to fit this category more often than not, as it is
what society has expected of them. Men, on the other
hand, have their own troubles with imbalance, often
fitting the stereotype of income earner, supporter, the
strong or unfeeling one. Neither way is good or bad. In
general, both are out of balance, however.

Both the female and the male aspects of society
have been out of balance, and the way to balance them
is to balance these qualities within ourselves first, then
we will see them manifest in the world. Self matters, we
must take care of ourselves first. We must, or nothing
works. You'll notice that on an airplane passengers are
always instructed to put the oxygen mask on themselves
first, for what good are you going to be to your children
if you're passed out?

When we drain ourselves of our lifeblood, tap ourselves dry, and ignore our needs, we are of no good to anyone else. We may be very strong, but over time we become sick, whether physically, emotionally, mentally or spiritually. When things have finally become so bad that we ask for help, it becomes clear we have chosen harmony over truth… but is it real harmony or the semblance of harmony? The place may look perfect, the job may look perfect, the family may look perfect, but we may be spinning our wheels trying to keep up the appearance of harmony, even when there might be several elephants in the room.

Eventually we realize this is not working, this is not harmonious, and we begin our search for truth. We begin to find out who we truly are, what our needs are, and that we need to take care of ourselves in order to help and love others. We begin our journey back to our Authentic Selves and authentic relationships.

True relationships exist where people are called on to look at their imbalances from a place of love, so that they may correct these imbalances and live a more fulfilled life. I like to live with authentic people, and the best quality I see in them, and the most loving one, is that when they see an imbalance in me that I am not aware of, they have the love and the courage to bring to my consciousness that which I need to work on in order to grow and evolve. Once we see the truth and start our journey back to ourselves we begin to become empowered again. We realize the only things we have control over in our life are our own choices, and as we begin our journey back to health, and to ourselves, others may follow our example, or they may not. Usually, over time, they will release their ego attachments that have held them in fear, control, and worry and choose love and authentic relating, too.

The power of a loving authenticity

I always say that if we all followed what was right for us, we would all be Home already, for what you do for yourself from your Authentic Self, serves not only you, but all others. It gets everyone Home faster. When we do not call people on their abuse and imbalances, we are not helping them or us. This is not love. Do for yourself what you would do for others. What is more important: a sense of false harmony or true balance and harmony?

Sometimes you have to make the hard choices for someone else that you would want made for yourself. You need to put up a boundary, rebalance something out of balance, leaving abuse and codependent patterns behind. This may not be easy at times, but if you love this person as much as you love yourself, you will be willing to risk losing them or never see them again, so you will do what is right for both of you. I had a tough decision to make in a situation having to do with someone so close and dear to me. I saw that the person was lost, angry, and going down the drain, and I had to make a decision to help him, as it would be what I would have wanted this person to do for me. So I had this beautiful being removed from me and taken to get help. I knew this meant that he might never understand my actions, might never want to speak or see me again. I was okay with this, for I knew it offered him an opportunity to find himself, his compass, and to journey back home to himself. I was blessed that he had the strength and courage to do his work and the subsequent healing. I think he understands that this experienced helped him be *him*. I think it helped him understand that the journey inward into self-discovery is the journey of true peace, love, and balance. He also helped me become more me. We danced this loving dance together.

GRATITUDE: Find what you are grateful for. Thoughts create our reality. What a better way to open your heart and change your life? We become, and our world becomes, what we focus on, so if you focus on gratitude then you will have more gratitude in your future. I practice every evening before going to bed, and many times throughout the day, finding something I am grateful for, something beautiful that is or has happened on that day. Even on the most difficult of days, I can always find something to be grateful for: a kindness, a beautiful sunset. Practice feeling what you want to create now, find it in your heart now, feel it now, and it will blossom in your future. If you can do this from a place of Unity, you will always create a world in harmony with the earth and with others. Let's start changing the world now, one at a time. We are incredibly powerful Beings, let's create a better world for all NOW.

ATTITUDE: This is the key to life. You can choose to be happy or not. You can choose to be in drama, to be the victim, or not. Or you can choose to take your power back, to give back what does not serve you. Do you want to keep dragging around all the abuse, the hurt the pain or suffering? Give it back! No one ever had the power to make us feel bad. We choose to feel and we are human but you can now become empowered and deal with those pieces, heal them within yourself, the plot or who did what to whom do not matter. Choose to heal.

Put the poison and the weights down and become Free. Live your life fresh and clean and clear today.

Choose to be happy. You cannot control the world around you, but you can control how you feel about it, whether to react to it or not, whether to let it take your power and your joy. If you know that nothing outside of yourself has the power to derail you, to make you feel not good enough, then don't let it happen. You are beautiful. Don't let anyone tell you otherwise.

Begin now to love yourself, to take a chance, to jump in and be free to choose to Love over everything else. Your life will be transformed, for you will begin to see that everything in your life is there for a reason and it will lead you Home. Knowing this makes the harder times more bearable, since we will be able to see the light shining through.

Find your peace in these moments, choose to see with your heart, ask for clarity as to why these things are in your life. Don't blame others; if something is in your life, it has meaning for you. You can only control your reactions to it and your feelings about it. So focus on how YOU wish to be. You are in charge of your life, so choose Love over fear, worry, revenge, resentment, hurt, abuse, judgment, and you will find the Joy, the Laughter and the Peace you so yearn for.

You'll find these divine gifts in *you.*

CHAPTER 3

BECOMING ONE

Did you ever have a day where everything was vibrant, shiny, and alive? I've had such a day, twenty-four hours where everything was luminescent, with a golden glow about it. I have a son who has been my greatest teacher; I am so grateful that he is in my life, for myriad reasons. He came home to visit one day, and we sat around the living room with his siblings, chatting. The room became vibrant and shiny as my son asked, "Mom don't you ever worry about what people think of you and who you are?" And I answered, "Honey if I worried about what people thought of me, I wouldn't be me, I would be what I thought they might want me to be." He said, "I really think I am starting to get that. Also, I find that when I meditate like you I go to this place were we are all One, and I am beginning to know things about people before they say things to me." I said, "It is a gift, use it wisely

*and for the good." Hearing these words from my child,
who once had many issues with my work, was like a cool
breeze, a breath of fresh air, like life and Spirit coming in.
From that moment on, everything was luminescent; every
material thing around me had a glow to it.*

What is meant by "Becoming One"?

Becoming One is about becoming Whole, it is finding the universality in all of us. What holds us together as One? What is the one thing we all have in common? What is the thing that makes us all the same?

The one thing we all have in common is Spirit. We have forgotten this. We are fractured, splintered, divided, and separated from what created us and where we came from. It is about figuring out who's the boss. The boss is not the voice in our head. That is only a piece of who we are. The whole truth is that we are a piece of God, of Source, of Creation. When we realize that, we discover who the boss really is. When we have become still long enough to connect to ourselves, to the whole part of ourselves, we discover the part that has not forgotten and is One with God, that is and will always and forever be the only true boss.

We come to this realization, first as it applies to

ourselves, but as soon as we become awakened to this fact, we come to realize that all humans and everything that has ever been created are also 'One.' In this chapter we will address individual places where we as humans have forgotten this piece, and speak about others that came into being to assist us in remembering, such as religion. If you do your own individual internal work and have Eyes to See, your "awakened eyes" will lead you to the true teachings that are at the core of many religions. But these eyes will also show you the places where religion is still separate and not whole, where manmade constructs have gotten in the way and created separation. The journey through religion to God is a valid pathway in conjunction with the awakened inward path. Wherever you are, whether you are in a temple, a church, a mosque, in nature, or sitting at home, take the time to find the Universal, the one thing that connects us as One, to Source, to God.

Why did we separate?

Long ago, in a meditation, I was shown the creation of time and space and that it occurred when Source had the desire to experience Love. In order to experience Love, the giving and receiving of it, duality had to be born. The world of opposites and polarities was born from a place of separating from the Whole, from the Creator. It was all an illusion, as there is no real separation, but we began to believe in this illusion so strongly that we forgot it wasn't real.

This illusion became very real to us, and we became very lost. We began to look at life as separate, asking *What is in it for me?* I believe that space and time were then created, so linear learning and inner evolvement could go hand in hand, until we once again awaken from the dream, whereupon time will cease and we will be consciously aware of our Oneness with our Creator.

This process is to continue until we become enlightened and actively embody the light within ourselves again, then Heaven on Earth will become our new reality. I believe this is what the Maya call "the end of time." It is not that the world comes to an end, but that so many become awake enough to realize that there is only the Now, and that nothing exists outside of it.

What could be more loving than to choose to give up our sovereignty in this place called earth, where this separation seems so real, in order to Become One again? To freely be of service to others and ourselves and to love thy neighbor as thyself?

I believe we all experience this very dense reality of earth, where we have to have a lot of courage, a lot of strength, where we experience much pain, until we realize we don't have to experience this reality any longer. We find acceptance for things, as we see they are "perfect," for they show us the way Home, back to our true self. We find that these experiences, as hard as they were, were only there to help us.

Jim proves it's never too late

I believe that each thing a person experiences and each path he or she chooses is perfection for them. It is futile to discuss which is the "right" path, for every path is "right," so if you choose to be an Atheist, a Jew, a Christian, a Muslim, a Buddhist, or none of the above, it is all perfect. I believe that before we come into this world we review where we are in our spiritual evolution and we pick the people in our lives and the events and the lessons that might help us evolve. Often these come in the form of pain or suffering or crisis, as we have discussed. It is in these times that we tend to look for answers and so often it is when we go within for an answer that we finally hit the jackpot!

It brings such a smile to my face when I have someone in session with me who is finally able to realize *God,*

I am not a complete and utter failure! For once they are able to look at their inner work and their spiritual development, and are able to see that these "setbacks," or mistakes in their lives were actually blessings, true gold mines. Sometimes this realization may take a while. I have been blessed to experience the moment where the light bulb goes on and they then have Eyes to See, perceiving their whole life, often for the first time, seeing how every interaction and every piece has led them to this moment of realization. The amount of love that pours in with this transfiguration is immense, palpable; the Love in the room is indescribable.

I had a man named Jim come to me, a beautiful man with a brain tumor, who was about to pass from this earth. His wife, a doctor, had brought him to me to see if he could find some peace beforehand, and some understanding as to why this was happening. When the moment of realization came for him, it was extraordinary. I remember him saying to me, "Avis, why is it now, as I end my life, I get it? Why only now do I understand it all?"

Why now? And in that same moment he answered himself.... for he could see what an impact he had had on others and would have on others, and how even his becoming awakened to this truth would, in turn, help others. He knew that even if he was to pass from this physical existence, the Love and his Love will always and forever be. Jim became aware that he had always known this, that he just happened to remember it now.

He knew that in the Now moment we are all One, we are not separate, and we will always be together, even though we may pass from this reality. He knew he was still here in the heart of everyone and everyone was in his heart. His passing over a period of many days was the most beautiful thing I have seen. He was surrounded by his loving family and friends. I feel blessed to have been part of his and his family's life.

Our choices between lives

I believe that before we are born we figure out where and with whom we will incarnate and what experiences we will have that might assist us in our evolution to becoming One again, to remembering who we truly are. So give thanks to the people in your life, especially those who have pushed your buttons, even those who have given you heartache and pain. For in the giving out of roles in this life, who do you think had the harder role to choose when it came to your evolvement at this time? Yes, the ones who supported you, loved you, and saw who you are from the beginning, even when you could not see yourself, had the easier roles.

I think the ones closest to us and the ones who caused us the most pain are the ones who also love us deeply and fully, for they loved us enough to come in to play the unpleasant role, even the "bad" role. So now, when someone or something pushes my buttons, I no longer blame him or her for what they are doing to me. This prevents me from going straight into the victim mode, since I realize that what is happening is about teaching me something, it is about remembering, and has nothing to do with them.

I get that this piece, what is happening now, is Divine and getting me Home, despite how it feels at the moment.

Here's how I handle it when I feel someone beginning to push my buttons. First I have to regain my composure. Only then can I start asking questions about what this is trying to tell me. What part of me is still in separation? Or what part of me still needs work and healing? What part of me is still wounded, feels unloved and unlovable?

I then can consciously begin taking responsibility

for what is appearing in my life and the direction my life is headed.

J.C. Penney got it right

Everything in our lives is here to teach us and to take us Home, and Home is literally where the Heart is. "It's all inside," we are reminded by the J. C. Penney slogan. The kingdom of Heaven is within; it is found within you. It is in your Sacred Pure Heart. The path of the Heart is where we become One with ourselves and with everything. I believe that once we find this place within us our only true desire becomes Love and Service. To me there is nothing else. It is the only real thing I know at this moment.

One aspect of being in service, for me, is to assist others, as I have been assisted, in remembering and awakening. We are coming to, and are in a time of rapid change and awakening. This is available to everyone, and as it is in everyone; all we need do is look WITHIN.

One thing I am so grateful for is that I have learned that truth is ever evolving and changing, depending on where you are standing and your perspective. Those stands of mine, those places where I hold my view, are always in the process of evolvement to a higher truth as I come to peace in understanding that everyone is always right *from their perspective.* I think that is why we have so much war. Both sides feel they are right...and they are. It is our job now to understand and appreciate another's journey as right and perfect, and to find a place that Unites us, not separates us.

We need to find forgiveness for the past, for we have all hurt and been hurt. We need to find acceptance for each other, to see the beauty in each and every individual. To find Unity. So please bear with me, for the words I share with you I share from the deepest part of me and with the most Love and Wisdom that I know at this time. I have come to learn that the more I know, the more I know nothing, so if any of my words help you on your journey home, I am eternally grateful. And if some of my words seem simple, rudimentary, and without merit, then please, please disregard them, I do not take offense.

Who's the boss?

Though the separation of mind and spirit happened so long ago, I think all of us, at some level, remember what it felt like to be "One," to have our minds and hearts united as One, and how it felt like Home. I think we are yearning to return to the Harmony, Love, Light,

Peace and Freedom of how that felt, the Grace. It is as if
we know we are missing something, a piece of ourselves
that we somehow cannot find, a piece of ourselves that
we have been looking for in this outside world and have
not found it, no matter how hard we try.

The truth is, we will never find it in the outside
world, in this world of duality, for what we are yearning
for is Unity Consciousness, and on this plane that lives
only in our heart, inside of us. In that time of Unity, so
long ago, before we separated, our hearts and minds
worked as one, in balance and whole, and we manifested
from that place of Unity. So anything we manifested was
always Whole, Balanced, and in service to All.

At that time, everything became manifest from
the heart, and therefore from the Unified Field, and
always served all, for we truly loved our neighbors as
ourselves.. Because we were One with our neighbor,
we would never create something that was solely for
us individually, or would hurt or create lack for our
neighbor or others.

At the present time, however, the mind and linear
thought have taken over, leading to separation from
the heart, polarizing our world, as our thoughts, our

creations, our greed and selfishness are in control.

The heart is One Unified Field, while the mind is split. The mind is dual and is devoted to separation, so any creations or manifestations from the mind will inevitably and inherently lead to separation. This means that if we are creating from the mind, a divided field, we are creating for ourselves and no others. So if we create abundance for ourselves, it is inevitable that we are creating lack for someone else. This separation is leading to the destruction of ourselves and our planet.

We, who are now creating from the split field of the mind, or of the ego, must regain our Spirit and our Heart, bringing them into balance with our mind. We must find our Compass.

We have become so divisive that we kill in order to maintain what is ours, versus what is theirs, to maintain our sovereignty at any cost, leading to hatred, division, war, and separation. We do so often with the mistaken conviction that we are right and they are wrong, that God is on our side, that we alone know the right way, with both sides convinced that God is siding with them. We do not understand that we are but One, and when we kill it is just as if the left arm were cutting off the right hand.

As we speed up, we make a slow discovery

We are only now, slowly, starting to understand that what we do affects absolutely everyone, that we are intricately connected, and that what we do as a nation, whether financially or ethically, affects everyone around the world. We are starting to discover our need to cooperate, even if we do so from a selfish understanding that the act of dumping on others eventually comes back to dump on us.

Because the world is speeding up, the time between our dumping on others and it zooming back at us is shortening, as we begin to learn that We are but One. What we do to others we do to ourselves, so what are you going to be doing? In other words, how do you wish to treat yourself? For it is that very decision that will come back to you.

We can no longer live in the world as if we are separated, as it becomes more and more clear that we all affect each other, that we are indeed connected, and what goes around goes around.

I believe all religions began with the same purpose: to help us find our Spirit, to reconnect with the Divine, to lead us to living a Sacred Life. A lot of the people mentioned in our bibles, torahs, and sacred texts, had this power, the power of Spirit. They were intimate with this power. Many of them left us words and texts along the way, describing how we, too, are to "become One" with Source, knowing that we have become unconscious, we are asleep, we have fallen from grace. We have drunk from the tree of knowledge, instead of drinking from the Tree of Life. We have been split, we have been separated, we have become dense, we have forgotten who we are, that we always will be One.

Our journey at this time is to remember this, to return home to Spirit. Where do you suppose Spirit lives? Not outside of us, but inside of us. So where are we to find Spirit, in our churches and temples, or inside of us? Religion is here to point the way, but we must go inside to find Spirit. Once it is found, we must use discernment in order to see what in our sacred texts is Divine and what is manmade.

The purpose of Spirit is to Unite, not separate, and unfortunately this message has been lost by a lot of religions. Many religions hold that they are the "only" road home and the only road to God, and if you do not follow their way, you will not make it home, since everyone who is not of that religion will be excluded from the kingdom of Heaven.

Even as a child it never made sense to me that God would choose one person or people over another. Does that seem Godly to you? How about a better idea: that all religions are okay, if you use your compass and your discernment to weed through to the words that are Divine as opposed to the words that are there to control.

Telling the Divine from the manmade

For me, it is so easy to see anything that unites as full of Love, equality, and justice, and that is Divine. On the other hand, anything that is in place to separate, to control, to exclude, to shun or hate others is manmade. With that said, the universe will provide exactly what you need in order to wake up and find your Spirit, and sometimes these questions, and these places, are exactly the catalyst for you to start finding your way Home. Every path is valid and perfect for each person. Religions all have one key component, something similar to: "The kingdom of Heaven is within," "the Lord is One," "God and everything are One, "We are all connected," "Know thyself," "Be still and know that I am," and "I am that I am." That is where so many valid religions carry the same truths. I haven't studied these texts enough, but I know the message is the same, and the message is in us. All the roads Home have a similar truth in them, disguised with different outer appearances, but all with the same message: Find yourself and you find Spirit, and you find Divinity, as we are all equal and we are all created in the image of God.

I personally believe that my body is my temple and God is within, so wherever I go God is with me. I don't personally need to go to a church, a temple, or a sacred place to find God… God is…and is with me. I personally feel that many religions do great works in the world, supplying shelter, food, support, community, and more, at the same time as they very often separate, exclude, control, and shun people. So I tend to stay away, since such exclusion and separation does not feel loving to me. It feels as if it is all about power over others.

But I can understand how it is helpful for some to find such refuge, prayer, and community on their journey, so it is a right path for so many, as are so many other paths. Finding Spirituality, though, remains an individual journey, not communal, and found only within. Once found within, it can be shared and amplified externally with others.

I believe, as so many of the texts indicate, that if you are to become Whole, become Fulfilled, and become One with Spirit, you will take that inward journey. Externals can only show you the way, but for the inward journey you travel alone. So often I see religious people doing all the right things, going to church, temple, following all the rules and regulations, but doing so without spirit or passion, functioning by rote, as if these actions on their own will lead them Home.

Zombie meditation won't work

If you are not present in your practice, and you do it by rote, without intent, purpose, or meaning, and without Spirit, it will not lead you to Spirit, but away from it. The opposite of what it was meant to create is what happens as you disconnect from Spirit. The people who handed these rituals down did so, if they had Divine intent from the beginning, in order to assist you in finding God. However, if you just follow them like a robot or a zombie, because you are "supposed to," if you only follow to fit in, you might find comfort in this but you will not find Fulfillment.

We have to EXPERIENCE the teachings, make them come alive, make them relevant to our life today. Once we experience them, we become One with them, we become en-light-ened, we begin living a Sacred Life, a life of Service, a life of Unity with all there is. The teachings are alive; take the time to become still and FEEL what they are trying to say and convey. Reading about them will only take you so far; you must take the time to do the Work so you will have Eyes to See and Experience what all those masters and teachers experienced themselves.

What rules and regulations do you think are man-made and which ones do YOU think are Divine? Go in to find YOUR answers, your truth, not the so called "truth" in the texts or the opinions of others. Use these opinions and texts to see if they speak to your heart and resonate with you and what you believe to be true deep inside your soul, not just what you were taught to be truths.

So many religious holidays carry so much impressive Spirit. However, they are so often celebrated without intent, meaning, or passion. I remember the first Passover dinner I had with people who came from a fairly religious Jewish background, at a time when I had just finished studying the Passover holiday. We went through the Passover Haggadah entirely, rushing through it in Hebrew with little English explanations for so many hours. Clearly everyone was just intent on getting through it. It was obvious that it had been done this way so often, the participants were hardly conscious of what they were saying. Everything was done in perfect Hebrew and everything was completed without skipping over anything; however, I believe we skipped over the most important element: being present to the story and its impact on us today, seeing what the journey and the story were about and what we learn from it and its impact on our lives today. How is it still alive and relevant to us today? Where were the passion and the Spirit? Passover is so alive to me, and relevant.

We come into this world enslaved, just like the Jews in Egypt. We may not realize it, but we are still slaves, caught in duality, for we do not know who we are, we have forgotten what binds us as One. It is only over time that we discover this fact, that we are trapped, slaves to illusion, and then we begin the journey to find out who we are and why we are here. On the way to discover Spirit, we find we *are* Spirit, we are One and always have been One, and thus we become Free. From this place of freedom, of becoming One with Spirit, we then choose to become One with God, we choose to be of service to God, and to me this is exactly the story of Passover and the relevance of Passover.

Finally, our Awakening

"Thy will be done." It is as if we become truly free, and from this free place we choose to serve the One. Even Elijah, to me, represents the spirit that is already present at the table, though so many cannot see. Elijah is within each and every one of us. He is the Messiah within, present at our table, just waiting to be awakened in each and every one of us. My message is that these myths and stories may point the way, but we have to do the Work, we have to go in and find the meaning for us, personally and individually. So, if religion is your path to the Light, to God, just make it your own, be present to the messages that are alive even today, find the true magic within the texts and within you, find the ones that resonate with you, the ones that speak to you, the ones that offer insights—and then bring them to life. They will remain asleep as long as you are asleep. They need you to be Awake and Present to become One with you and alive, for in that place of Unity you both carry Spirit. Find Spirit within it and within yourself, don't let it pass you by, practicing by rote while remaining asleep.

As this revolution happens to us, one by One, it's our Awakening. It is the New Earth. I believe that old tired structures, including some religions that each proclaim to be the only one with a pathway to God and salvation, will begin to grow into their original teachings, which showed that the way is possible and attainable by all, not just for some. It will no longer be a world where only some can be saved, the others damned. Rather, universal teachings will be revealed, raising cultural flares where diversity is embraced and cohesiveness maintained, all united by One common bond— our Humanity, our Divinity and our Love.

All paths are valid and all roads lead to Home, but when you get Home, you find it is a state of Being, not a place, a state of becoming One with your Creator, with your Divinity, and with God. You get there by being present and going within. It is in this place of Being where the path disappears; everything disappears, and the world is seen for what it truly is - an illusion. We begin to see that "nothing matters," as one reaches this place, except for Love. We become more tolerant of others and their ways, we become more accepting, less judgmental, non reactive, and we truly begin to see we are all One. This is not a destination or a place, but a state of Being, a way of Being. It becomes a way of life, the Sacred Life.

The Masters taught empowerment, not ritual

I think what may have happened to the teachers and masters that we know of, such as Buddha and Jesus, is that after they attained a state of enlightenment, people would write about how they did it, and these writings became the torahs, the bibles, the writings about their life, and ultimately the religions. The problem, I think, is that the Masters intended that their teachings empower people and show them the way, that their teachings become alive in each person, showing them one path to follow, one of many.

Instead, each religion ritualized their lives and made the path the religion, instead of the teachings, which were Universal. This then made the path very structured and it lost its life force. The rituals became the important thing, rather than the teachings. In other words, we started to let religion's texts become idols, forgetting the true meaning and true teaching. The texts were meant to be a guideline for "experiencing" spirit, teachings that become alive within us, experienced with intent, purpose, passion, and presence, not passive teachings,

People, not all, but many, followed the ritual, but forgot its original intent. Each Master had an initiatory path that might help others attain the same state. But it also might not, for someone else's path may require something completely different, and that is why all paths are valid: There as many paths as there are beings on this planet.

Someone said it to me this way the other day. "It is as if a person becomes enlightened, and the grandchild experiences what it's like to be around this person and writes about how the person lived and how they attained enlightenment, and that becomes the religion. Soon the important thing becomes the story, not the inner path."

Somehow we missed the point. I am not saying religion isn't a good thing, I am just suggesting that we be present in our practice, that we practice with intention. Discern what feels manmade and what feels Divine, what is Love, what creates Love, and what is fear, worry, or hatred, creating more hatred and separation. What piece is manmade out of duality, and what is Divine and pure Love?

I truly believe that the masters of old were trying to tell us how they achieved enlightenment or how they became One with God. When Jesus said, "I and the father are One," I think he meant he had become One with his creator, and that we too could do this. "The kingdom of Heaven is within," he said, and "Of myself I can do nothing." I think he meant *Go within and find out who you are, for you will find your Divinity and become One with it. Be a part of something greater than yourself.* He also saw that we, too, could do this and more.

So I think his point was not to create a religion, but instead a pathway of internal initiation leading to Oneself, to Unity and to all that is and is not. I think he meant it as a way to find out who you are, via a journey of self-discovery that will lead us Home.

I believe that our teachers and masters tried to convey to us the way that they become more Enlightened, how they gained at-one-ment, and that they meant to establish a guideline. I think that if they saw us dispassionately following the things they did or told us to do, without being present and without going inward, they would say we missed the message. One thing they all had in common is that they found "it" inside of them. So it doesn't matter where and how your path leads you, if at some point you go within to become your own teacher, for then you will be the greatest Teacher of all.

Go wherever you find the Light

I truly feel my body is my temple and God is within,

so wherever I go God is with me. I do not need to go anywhere to find God; God is in me, as it is in everyone. If you find that you access your place of finding God more consciously in the woods, in a temple, or church, or in the water, then follow whatever brings you closer to the light. At some point, in this place where you feel more connected, close your eyes and see the translucence and beauty of who you truly are and the beauty of others.

Self does matter, and I think this is what people mean when they say, "We are the Ones we have been waiting for." For yes, you have been waiting for You, YOU ARE THE ONE. It has always been You. In some religions it is the Holy Ghost, in another it could be Elijah at your table. You are your own savior, and you are the One you have been waiting for.

Working with the shadow

Part of becoming One and discerning "who's the boss" is working with our shadow and the hold it may have over us. The shadow work is about bringing our light and our dark into balance. Our shadow is all those parts of ourselves that we have denied, that we think are not "good" enough, all those parts of oneself we have repressed in order to fit in and in order to be loved. In reality, our shadow is "good," as is everything else; it serves the light and it takes us Home, but only when we acknowledge its existence by allowing ourselves to hear it. So often it carries gems of information about what we're seeking: our true self.

For instance, very often when someone pushes our boundary, yells at us, or hurts us, our immediate instinct is to react and yell back, to correct the wrong or address the injustice. But often we repress this reaction, swallow it, and bury it deep, because we don't want to rock the boat, or we just want to fit in, or we have been told that getting angry is not a good thing.

Getting angry can be a very good thing; it is very often your compass itself, telling you something is wrong. It can be sending a message to someone to back off, that they have pierced your boundary, that you are being treated abusively. Anger is always telling us something. Our work is to remember that it is in our life for a reason, even though it may be part of our shadow that we want to repress, since it doesn't feel good and we don't want others to see it. Understand that it may be trying to alert us that something is wrong, off, and off balance.

Suppressed anger's unpleasant surprise

Why not avoid anger? Because if you suppress, if you don't address your anger, it will come out when you least expect it, at the craziest of times, in the least appropriate situations and places. Even in that case, the shadow is still trying to help you by saying, "You see this crazy thing you just did that made no sense? Please, please look at it, for here is a clue to who you are."

We often talk about anger over spilled milk. I remember one day, when I was a child, some milk spilled on the floor and the reaction of one particular adult was completely over-the-top and out of balance. How could this milk have caused all this emotion and pain by just spilling out on the floor? Even as a ten-year-old I realized this reaction had nothing to do with the milk on the floor, it had to do with some previously unaddressed hurt, problem, injustice, or imbalance, so now what should have been addressed so long ago is being directed at the milk or anyone around the perimeter of the milk. Whatever has not been addressed has magnified in force and become a demon brought to life, a living monster ready to come out when you least expect it.

Be grateful when this happens, for it is you trying

to help yourself, asking you, *Wow, where did that come from? Maybe I need to go back to see what is causing this crazy reaction, why I am feeling this way!*

There are two types of anger, the first is a natural reaction to an incident or words spoken that have crossed your perimeter or boundary. The most loving way to deal with this, is to address it at the moment, when possible, by responding with your version of, "You have crossed my boundary. There has been an attempt at breaching my perimeter, and I do not like it, neither will I put up with this kind of behavior in the future." This is addressing a problem in the moment, meeting whatever force came at you with the same matching energy, in order to stop it, wake up the person, and not enable out-of-balance behavior.

Spirit without a halo

I always say Spirit doesn't always look "angelic," and sometimes it can look like the terminator! If the terminator is coming at you, then you have to meet it with its own level of energy in order to stop it, to bring it into balance. You have to speak its language in the moment in order to get through. Eventually the important piece, as you come into Balance and become Whole, is that while you may be acting like the terminator, even yelling, in order to place a boundary around yourself, really it is coming from a place of Peace and Love inside yourself.

Jesus in the temple had to display anger and yell in order to stop an event. He had to meet the force coming at him with the same force given back, but as soon as he dealt with it he turned to the child next to him and was again sweet and docile.

The second kind of anger is repressed anger, and this, I think, is much more insidious. This is anger held back from addressing an incident at the moment it happened, such as the milk incident above. Instead of reacting by voicing your reaction and saying to the person at the time, "This is how your words or actions made me feel i.e.: sad, not good enough, hurt, etc…" we suppress it and it begins to have a life of its own. You can feel this just below the surface of some people, everyone can sense this anger except the person who has it. And more often than not they blame others for everything, for they cannot possibly look at their shadow, as they believe they have to be perfect, and looking at this aspect of them makes them feel imperfect. They have repressed all "negative" feelings, so they are steeped in them and are ready to explode at any moment.

Try to remember your own hurts and have compassion for such people, because deep down inside, they are reacting like this because they have been hurt, because they feel unloved and abandoned. They need to be loved, and it will be your choice at some moment to comprehend this, to feel the Love and send them Love, either by the putting up of a boundary, or, more important, by conveying Love instead of anger and hatred.

They may be ready to heal and shift, in which case they may need Love and Compassion and kind loving words, rather than the energy of the terminator. It will be your call, and you'll do well to get still, breathe, be present, find the Peace and the Love inside yourself. Take three breaths and make your choice from there as to how to proceed in each and every situation. If you are at this stage, it probably means you have come to this level of compassion yourself by having journeyed this way earlier, and by finally looking at your shadow and learning and listening to what it is trying to tell you. It, too, is trying to tell you that you are Love.

Looking for Love in the dark

Once we start comprehending these pieces, and they are in each and every one of us, we begin to see with more clarity; we begin to see the Light in the dark, the Love in the dark, and we begin to help others heal this piece, too. At some point, as we become more en-light-ened, we find that eventually we no longer react to anything, as we see that it is all "good" and that it is all taking us Home. We realize that when these pieces appear in our lives we cannot blame others, for if they are appearing in our life they have a "good" reason to be there. We see that we can learn instead of blame.

These life events then seem more like watching Jerry Springer moments go by—witnessing them, but not engaging in them. We are able to accept everything as Divine and perfect in our lives, there to teach us, to open us up, and to bring us closer to the Light and to the Love. Every moment becomes a choice point. Will you choose fear and worry or will you choose Love?

How often do you see the shadow popping up in relationships, trying to help? There is the common dance in relationship where one person calls the other on an imbalance, and if the person receiving the comment is still in victim, or hurt mode, and cannot receive the information from where it comes, which is ultimately Love, but takes offense and sees it as a place where they are deemed "imperfect," or not good enough, then this is where an unfortunate dance often begins. The dance then becomes "Let me show them, they don't think I am perfect or good enough, wait till I show them all the places where *they* are not perfect! The person conducts a personal crusade to derail the other person, picking on everything they do or don't do. From here on in, something that was done out of Love, calling your partner on an imbalance, morphs into an all-out war.

Either way, whether you are the instigator or the receiver of this energy, know that it is still trying to tell you something about you, and that this, too, is Divine. If you are the instigator, stop! Go in and see where you are still wounded, hurt or feeling abandoned and reclaim your Power. Remember that no one has the power to make us feel unloved or victimized; we just allow them to make us feel that way.

You may have no control over what happens outside of you, but you do have control over how you react. So if someone is trying to derail you, choose to see the good in every situation and don't take things personally. If you know everything is "good" and is there to help, why get all caught up in it? Choose to see what is really going on underneath everything, and decide to heal and Love. Embrace your shadow side and all it has to teach you. Integrate all of you, the dark and the light, forgive yourself and all others, as it is your Road Home.

Welcoming a partner, not needing one

Another relationship that needs to come into balance is that between our masculine and feminine. Much has been said about the Divine Feminine, bringing her in and coming into balance with Her. Yes, this must be done as part of the journey into Wholeness, and into becoming One, but so is bringing the Divine Masculine into balance within us. For if the feminine is out of balance, it stands to reason the masculine is, too. So in our process of forgiveness, let's forgive both aspects of ourselves and come into acceptance, trust, and balance with this piece.

Once this balancing happens, then our *need* for an external relationship or partnership ceases. We do not need a partner any longer in the same way—we are Whole and complete. And this is exactly when a beautiful partner shows up in our life, should we desire it instead of needing it. Two wholes becoming One, instead of two halves becoming One. It could even be someone you have been in relationship with up until now, and all of a sudden you both hit the balance point and the relationship becomes glorious.

This is a Catch 22: When you release the need and the sense of lack, the relationship comes in, and I believe the relationships formed from this place are of a different nature. There are no power struggles, the person is free and not enslaved, and each partner is supportive of the other in myriad ways. And I do believe they are United forever.

So drink from the Tree of Life and release everything from the tree of knowledge. The way from one tree to another is through the spiritual path, the inner path: the Sacred journey of self-discovery and healing. It is from this path that we transcend this earth, as we become able to SEE everything, to see the LOVE in everything and everyone. We are able to see the true, Authentic Divine Being in everyone, while simultaneously acknowledging the masks, the imbalances, the dysfunction. We can look beyond to see the essential self.

We are all looking for the same thing: to be loved, to be forgiven, to be safe, to be nurtured, and to feel valued for who we are. Find that Sacredness within yourself, and you'll see it reflected in others and in your world. Once found, it will be with you forever; once found, you begin to understand the saying, "Nothing matters," for in a sense it doesn't. It is all in perfect order. It's all Love, and it all leads us Home. Once this sacredness is found, we choose Love and we choose Service. What could be better? It's Heaven on Earth right here right now.

So connect to your inner child, as she will guide you on the journey of Heavenly delights and Bliss. Don't get too serious, don't let fear and worry set in, for when we become too serious, we seriously lose our connection to Spirit. *Can you hear me now? Can you hear me now?* This is Spirit trying to connect. So get out of the way and allow Spirit to come through, allow the Love to come through.

Becoming One

What is "becoming One?" it is becoming One with all that is and is not, with God, with the Creator, with Source. We only find that place of Unity within us. "BE STILL AND KNOW THAT I AM," says the inner voice we hear in the quiet.

Many teachers have taught the way, the way of the path, the path within. I believe, from the innermost part of my being, that Jesus taught this way. His teachings were about how to become Whole again, retrieve our Divine spark within, and reunite with our Creator as

One. By doing so, we become One with God in his/her image. Jesus's teaching that we are all the children of God was not his exclusively. His teachings were meant to point the way and were never meant to be the basis for another religion, especially one that would be used so often to control, to maintain power and separation, and to take the path away from the individual, resulting in the antithesis of his teachings.

Instead, religion created the very obstacles and barriers that came between us and God, meant to control us and keep us from connecting directly to God. Religions often say: "You must go through us to reach God, you must follow our ways, they are the only way, everyone else is wrong, we have the only true way. You must follow the rules and commandments we tell you to follow, we will tell you what truth is, what to do and when to do it, and how to do it, sometimes even what to eat and not to eat, creating a separation between you and others."

Having to look for something outside of yourself, be it a rabbi or priest, a place, a church, or a temple to guide you in your life strips you of your own innate connection to God. Using these places in conjunction with your own guidance is one thing, always checking in with your own inner sense first, only then listening to others. Don't get me wrong, there are many incredible rabbis and priests and sages who can help you along the way to finding enlightenment and fulfillment, but discernment is utterly essential.

The ultimate taboo

Often in religious practice, connecting to God directly is considered taboo, a form of witchcraft, not to be done. Please tell me then, how do you explain the notables in the bibles and texts who connected to God directly, such as Moses, Abraham, and Jesus? They were certainly not labeled "bad," so why are we, if we are try to connect directly? Doesn't that seem odd and rather controlling?

Of course, mixed in with these religions' rules are valid teachings interspersed with the ones that are not, so it can be very deceiving. This is where you need to use your compass. Does it make any sense to you to believe in keeping yourself separate from others whom you don't accept, believing that your group is somehow the only recipient of God's Love and that no one else on the planet will receive God's grace? "If you do not follow us, you will be damned." How many religions espouse this?

I never understood how God could Love one over another, that his/her love was conditional, depending on what I did or did not do, or on where I was born and what I was taught. The belief that if I had been simply born in the wrong place and of the "wrong" religion I might not reach God, seems anathema to me. If every religion believes it is "right," how can they all be right? Doesn't this alone make them all wrong? Why can't they all be right, considering themselves just different paths that lead to the same place?

We are all human and as such we are One and created by One. God and us, we are One, created in his/her image. As such, we are all equal, with equal access to God, regardless of our religion, lack thereof, or where we were born. God is God, and God is Love, period.

Everything else is in duality, polarity, not Unity. You were created in the image of God, so where do you suppose you will find God? In You, of course.

The tools that get us to our final destination:

1) "Love your neighbor as thyself," for we are all One. How could you harm yourself? So treat others as you would treat yourself.

2) Accept what is. This does not mean condoning

what is, but accepting that "It is what it is." You cannot change it in the moment, so accept, while checking on how you choose to react, act, or witness it. If it is an uncomfortable moment, surrender, and know that the Universe has bigger plans for you. Allow the Universe to navigate you to where you need to go. Let go of judgment as to what is "good" or "bad" in the present moment; it is all Divine and taking you home.

Stay present, stay awake, don't go unconscious and fall "asleep." Everything is an opportunity to evolve, to grow, and to learn, *if you embrace it.*

3) Forgive yourself and others. As with acceptance, this does not mean condoning or even having dinner with someone.

4) Express your Gratitude at all times. *Ahhhh!* This is the quickest way to feel the Love and the fastest way to bring more Love into your life.

5) Your thoughts create your reality. So what are you thinking? Not just now, but all the time? Being present to your thoughts will move you out of this illusion, out of this world of time and space and into Unity, the only thing that is truly real. Unity is the place where you came from, where you are now and where you will

always remain, at Oneness.

We are asleep and in a dream, and we need to remember who we are, why we are here, and what we came here to experience: duality and separation. Are you on the return journey Home, or are you falling deeper into the dream? Are you ready to wake up from the dream? Have you experienced enough lack, pain, and suffering? Have you learned enough lessons and ready to choose Light and Love and Unity once again, now from a much more evolved conscious level?

You are truly a choice faced with a choice. Choose to become One and change your life for the better, forever, NOW.

CHAPTER 4

CRISIS

What will you choose when crises appear? Will you become the victim one more time, sighing, "Here we go again, the world and everyone in it is not trustworthy, they will all hurt me and abandon me eventually"? Will you choose to perpetuate the imbalance, the dysfunction, the tired old patterns, or will you choose Happiness, Balance, true Harmony and Love in your moments of crisis? Will you find your voice and choose Kindness? Or will you remain unconscious and choose fear and worry and blame? Will you choose to remain separate? Or will you take the time to remember?

What is crisis? Crisis is OPPORTUNITY. Crisis announces *It's time for change, time to learn, time to evolve.*

It took me a long time to learn to look at a crisis as

an opportunity to grow, instead of a time of despair, a time of blame, pain, and suffering, fear and worry. My husband, Joel, always reminds me to use the moments when we or others appear to have failed, or fallen down, as a time to talk, a time to assess where we are, and a time to decide to make choices about our future from a conscious place. This can be an opportunity to let Grace come into our lives!

If you have children, a crisis that involves them is the perfect time to talk, to teach, a time for them to listen to what you have to say, especially if they've lost the right to not listen in that moment. They won't be as likely to get up and run if there might be consequences for their recent actions; they will be on their best behavior. But be sure to speak from the Heart so they are able to feel your concerns and the LOVE you have for them.

Have you ever noticed how present you are during a time of crisis, how introspective you become, and how it turns into a time of evaluation and reevaluation of past choices in preparation for moving forward with more Grace, Balance, and Love? Do you take the time during a crisis to find your inner voice, speak from the Heart, and make choices that are more Balanced, Kind, and Loving?

Crisis is an opportunity for change that can be liberating and empowering. A crisis happens when something is trying to be birthed— YOU! It's you trying to come out, to become Whole, it is your soul speaking to you, a time to quiet down, be still, and listen. What is Spirit trying to tell you? Crisis is a time of insight, if you are willing to breathe, be still, lower your defenses, become vulnerable and honest with yourself, and go inside for guidance. At these times, you discover what it is you wish to change; you discover what truly matters, what is important to you; the kind of environment you wish to live in, what kind of world you want to live in, and what kind of world you want to create. It is a time of building your future and it is an opportunity to build a better world.

Crisis can be what finally tears the veil

Use crisis as a learning point, an opportunity to assess where you are, to address imbalances and abuses, to make choices that empower you and others. If your immediate reaction is to blame others for a failure or for the crisis, you missed the lesson. What is this crisis trying to teach you? If you had to speak from the Heart, what would this crisis bring out in you? It is an opportunity to grow, to wake up and to Love. Michael

Beckwith says, "Behind every human aberration is a spiritual aspiration trying to break through."

In my view, crisis can be a time where the veil breaks, light comes in past the ego, past the separation and past the imbalance, to reach LOVE. It is the time our Spirit is calling us to wake up, to retrieve our power and ourselves. Most often it is in these darkest moments that we find our most powerful insights, since crisis allows the inner voice, the Divine voice within us to come through and speak. Don't try to avoid the lesson. Instead, embrace it, it will only repeat and get worse if you do not.

As a mom, I wanted my children to avoid being hurt, until I realized that by shielding them I was keeping them from evolving, learning, and from the biggest gift of all, discovering who they truly are. For it is in these moments that we shed, release, and let the Light slide in. Crisis is our alarm going off, saying *Time to wake up*. In my own life, crisis has been "the best of times and the worst of times," for in those moments I have felt the most pain, but also the most Grace, connection, awe, magic, and wonder. It is in these moments where I have learned the most. Why? Because I took the time to be Present, to go inside, to Remember and to choose, to make decisions that lead to true Harmony.

Crisis can come in many forms, disease, physical pain, accidents, emotional heart wrenches, loss, spiritual vacuums, or angst, depression, anxiety, addiction. By the way, I so often think that all of us have some sort of addiction, for what do I think addiction is? To me it feels as if we are trying to fill this place inside of us; we are trying to feel good, feel grace, and feel whole. Addiction, whether it is to drugs, alcohol, food, shopping, sex, hoarding, whatever it may be, is the urge to become Whole, Complete, and Happy. The addiction, whether it's to shopping or having an orgasm, gives us that feeling of wholeness, just for a moment, an ever-fleeting moment, but then it is gone. After this we are in the ever-searching mode again, doing more and more of whatever the addiction consists of, in the hope that this time the good feeling will stick and be permanent, enabling us to maintain the state of Grace and of Wholeness. We know, however, that the only way to succeed at this is it is found inside of us, where it permanently resides and is waiting for us to Remember.

The only real reality

While addiction gives us glimmers of this feeling of Wholeness, it takes us further and further away from attaining true Wholeness. Each time the addiction hits full crisis point, we are given a new CHOICE point. Again: Will we choose the Love and Light found inside, or will we revert to the old pattern that keeps us separate and in duality and pain? Will we choose separation instead of Unity? Step off the world as you have known it, and into the world of the unknown and wander within, to find the deepest and most lasting of treasures.

I used to think that grace was found at the outer edges of our existence, in the place at the far right of balance, where ecstasy is found, but I found that as soon as the euphoric, ecstatic moment passed, the down side had to come with the swing of the scales. So ecstasy was quickly followed by sadness, regret, and pain. That is a description of living in duality, the place of opposites. It is an illusion, it is not real. There is another reality, the true reality, and it is the Unified Field.

We find this reality inside us; it is the place before the opposites, before duality, the place of Oneness and Unity. It is where we all came from and where we truly all are. It is very hard to explain, because it is out of the realm of time and space, and out of the realm of words. It is where we are One with our Creator and with everything that has been and has not been. It is the place of reconnecting and acknowledging the presence of the Divine spark within.

This is what we are all searching for in life, on our journey, often mistakenly looking for it in alcohol, drugs, shopping, sex and so on, thinking that these externals can give us this Grace. I realized that the place of Grace was not at the outer edges, but dead CENTER, within me and within you. So I began meditating and finding that center within, the place of BEING. I found it to be the place where nothing is black and white, where there is no cold nor hot, no good, no bad; it is the place of Source before duality, and after duality. It is the place of no time; it is the place of no space.

The day I finally gave up

I thought it was pretty funny, the day I finally gave up. It was the day of final crisis. I was ill, and in pain emotionally, physically, spiritually. I had been in pain for a long time, and no matter what I did, it just got worse. Despairing, I finally threw in the towel. I felt I had done all the "right things," everything my family, teachers, friends, and peers told me I should do in order to be happy and be loved. I thought if I just was good enough—with society, not I, deciding what "good" meant—I would be happy.

I had followed the rule book as I believed it, because I wanted to fit in and be loved. But as I woke up I came to understand that in compromising many of my beliefs, I had lost my ability to voice what I truly felt inside, and so had forfeited the ability to be my Authentic Self. Following what others told me to do no longer made any sense to me. I had lost my compass by trying to please others. I needed to Love myself, and make the best choices out of Love and for myself.

I learned that the only way to serve others is to serve ourselves from a place of Balance, a place of Authenticity and Unity. We are only One, so what we truly do for us, from a place of Love, Unity, and Grace serves all. So on that day, here I was in a heap of sadness, despair, on the cold bathroom floor begging for answers and relief, looking for guidance, in a complete meltdown, feeling soooo alone, so sad … *It's not supposed to be like this…* and then it happened.

It was as if a switch had been triggered within me…I felt the love as the light went on, and then, wow, everything I have always been looking for outside myself, all my life, I found within. It was always there, I had just forgotten. The key was inside of me, what a perfect hiding place! I had been sitting on a beach of gold and was unaware of it.

I came to realize then, as I do now, that we are on a journey here of self discovery, and in that journey of self discovery we finally come to remember who we truly are, what we came here to do.

What I found on the bathroom floor

We came here to discover and remember HOME and that we are all truly One as we discover our Divinity, our Breath, and our Life. We are in this together, we came in together we will go back together, each of us lighting the spark of Remembrance within, one at a time.

What I discovered and remembered that day, on my bathroom floor, was no less than Eternal Love and Unity. It was utterly indescribable. I knew in that moment that I was touching the part within my self, within all of us and everything, that we are searching for, the source that created us. It exists within every single person. What I felt was exactly the sense of *being* that we are here to experience, in order to become more compassionate, loving, empathic, and evolved.

We all have free will, and are free to choose to come Home, to be One with the Light again. I believe that our Creator, God, Source, Light, Nature—whatever it may be for you—

wished to experience Love, and so created separation, the only way to experience the giving and receiving of love. We were all part of that process, and now we are on our way back Home to the remembrance of Unity. But, in the meantime, we have forgotten who we are, what we came to do, and our true purpose in being here.

We became dense and caught up in our minds. We disconnected from the heart, we lost our way, our compass, our inner voice, our guidance system, we made this all real; we forgot it is all an illusion.

The good thing is that we have not taken any wrong turns. Every event that led to my being on the cold bathroom floor was perfect and absolutely filled with Love, even if I could not see at the time that it would lead me Home. Every person who interacted with me did so with Love, for they drew from me what needed to be found. I always say that our enemies and the people who have hurt us the most, carry the most love, for they are the ones who drive us inward, sometimes painfully, till we find ourselves and what we want in our lives.

These "enemies" help us in finding our Compass, our Balance. I see this happening in my sessions all the time. People arrive at my door so distraught, saying "I made the wrong choice, took the wrong turn, I went the wrong way. I failed!" But as we look into their journey during the session, I always find that there are no wrong turns. Everything is perfect and exactly the way it should be.

How often do you hear of people, even after they've been through hell in the form of one or more crises, say they would not go back to change a thing? I admit that to the outside, linear world, my own life choices may have seemed wrong, but I also know deep inside that they were perfect for me. The universe always gives us what we need in order to grow, to learn, to evolve, and ultimately to go home.

I think that we are getting ready to say we have had enough crises in our lives. We're at the stage now when we no longer automatically fall back asleep after the crisis, but remain awake more often. And now, when a crisis comes, we are able to see the light shining through almost immediately. This takes a lot of the pain and suffering away as we start seeing the crisis as something "good," as an opportunity that makes us more complete, more Whole, more directed.

The rewards of staying awake

Whenever I am in a transformational time—which is often a time of crisis—as I begin to feel the pain and suffering of the moment I try to not let myself fall asleep. Instead, I Remember. I look into my past, thinking of other times where I have been in crisis and pain. As I look back, something interesting happens: The hurt of the past no longer holds power over me, and there is no pain. I see, instead, where it has all led me, the good that came out of it, and how it formed me. I see where it took me, and realize that it always, inevitably and eventually, took me to the right place. These moments always brought me more Insight, Wisdom, Knowing, Healing and Wholeness and Love.

So now when I come to these moments I sit back and, instead of going into the pain, I say to myself, *I know this too will lead me to a better place, I know this too will pass, so why not shift how I feel about it now? I know and trust this is good and I know this piece is serving me and others, so why not feel the Love of that now? Why not choose to witness, to feel the Universe and*

God sending exactly what I need to accept, and feel the Love inherent in the moment? From this perspective, everything changes. We change and everything changes. When we change inside, everything changes.

When these moments appear now, I look at them as an opportunity, even as an adventure. When my finances went south, when I hit a crisis with finances, instead of going into victim mode, I thought, *Here is an opportunity, a move, a change in direction. Where is the Universe taking me? An adventure is beginning, I need to keep my eyes and my ears open, stay awake, look for signs, signposts, guidelines, and synchronicities.* When my finances tanked, I found our beautiful home, way beyond my dreams. I am grateful. I am just the guardian of this beautiful house for the time being. It came in our price range and it serves all of us in every way— my husband, my children, and me. Miracles do happen. I feel it to be a "gift from the gods," a gift from the Universe.

In times of crisis, we have the opportunity, we have the CHOICE to become more Divine, closer to God, closer to Love. It is in these moments that we can find the hope for change, and the hope for a better world, where no one is oppressed for any reason, be it by our race, or gender, our religion, or sexual preference. And we begin to believe that "We can be the change we want to see in the world." That we can remember who we are and that we are all One. That we have the capacity, deep in our soul, to create a better world where we treat each other with respect and we begin to live in a United world where everyone is equal and of equal value, like a puzzle in which we are all a puzzle piece, an integral part of the whole, each piece different, but of equal value and worth. Each one of us is a gift and a part of the Whole.

The best reaction to button-pushers

Crisis is choice: When our buttons get pushed, we can choose to do what we have always done in the past, which was to blame others, to become defensive, to argue until we prove we are right, and In that way continue to be in separation from ourselves and others, or we can choose to know that the Universe is sending us exactly what we need.

We begin to realize our experience doesn't have anything to do with any one else, but has all to do with us. So what is the universe trying to teach us and show us in these moments? It's this: Every time someone pushes our buttons it is an opportunity to look at the places where we still see ourselves as separate. It is time to see where we need healing, where we need self love and nonjudgment of ourselves and others. The crisis is asking: Where do we still feel imperfect, not good enough, not loved enough, abandoned? It is a time to look at our boundaries: Are we violating the boundaries of others, or are we letting others push through ours?

I always say that there are no good or bad people, just imbalance. If someone is pushing through your boundaries and you are allowing it, then you are enabling the behavior and perpetuating the pattern and the imbalance. The most loving thing to do is to give voice to the situation, to verbalize the imbalance and correct it. You can only do this for yourself; the other person may choose to listen, learn, and follow, or stay in the imbalance, stay in the anger, stay in the bitterness; they have a choice, too. Use your judgment as to how you will do this. If the situation is a dangerous one, using your voice may just mean removing yourself from the dangerous situation, choosing not to return to it, and perhaps choosing to go to professionals who can help you deal with a volatile situation.

Ask for help. You can do your part in correcting the imbalance by remembering that the only choice you have is your choice, you cannot control others and their choices, only your own.

So when someone pushes my buttons, (and yes they still get pushed) my automatic first reaction is to be stubborn, but these days I take a breath in order to Remember that there is only One of us here having this exchange, and not two people, and if so, what is the universe telling *me* about *me*? I find it is always telling me where I am still caught in the illusion of separation, where I am still in duality, where I am still asleep, and that it is time, time to Remember, and a time to heal. It is a time to understand that everything that has happened to me has had a purpose, has had a reason, that even the most difficult lessons and experiences were trying to reach me, trying to wake me up.

Seeing all the way to the Authentic

Looking back, I realize that my buttons being pushed has nothing to do with the present moment, but is zooming me back to an original wounding that happened so long ago. Today I can go back in time and ask that event *What do you have to teach me now that I was not ready to see feel or strong enough to experience then?* Even with the most painful of hurts, I go back and reassess my reaction to it and my perception of it.

If I can go in without judgment, with love for myself and the other person involved, I can see that they too have suffered, they too have been hurt, they too have been victims, that they too have had their boundaries pushed, and I see the imbalance and the separation in them and in myself. But now I start to see all the way to the true Authentic Being, to their true essence, acknowledging that the imbalance, the separation is just an illusion; it is not the real being. It is the dualistic, separate side of them and in me showing. It is their own unloved, out-of-balance self showing, and so I am able to release the event. I am able to forgive them and forgive myself. I am able to have compassion and empathy for myself and the other person or persons.

This is my time of choice. I can choose to stay in the imbalance, and perpetuate the hurt and anger, or I can use my eye—my Inner Eyes— to See, and choose to heal, letting it go into Love and Light, into Unity, and realize it was just an illusion.

When we carry these hurts into the future, they weigh us down. It is as if someone pointed a gun at us once, and we stopped breathing and never did breathe deeply again, even though the gun was put away and the danger and abuse ended! We were scarred, not

quite healed, and we carried the hurt with us wherever we went. We rejected the many opportunities the
Universe gave us to see it, heal it, and release it, every
time our buttons were pushed. Instead, we go on automatic pilot, trying to defend ourselves, trying to hide
the wound, concerned that if they see it they will know
we are imperfect, we will not be loved, we will not be
good enough.

But when we do our inner work, taking charge and
taking responsibility for our lives and our actions, we
begin to take control of the ship. We find our Compass,
we find our Captain and we find our true self again. We
begin to look at every experience as an opportunity and
a time to heal and a time to Love. This is the choice point
where we choose to no longer believe we are separate,
but that we are One. We see not only where the imbalance happened, but that whatever the imbalance was,
we have become part of it, we are it, and we keep it alive.

Stop! Give the poison back.

Someone gave us the poison—be it in the form of
neglect, abuse, criticism and so on—

and we took the poison in, deciding to carry it, endlessly poisoning others and ourselves.

Stop! Give it back, return it! It does not serve you any longer, become free! It is your choice to do this. Only you can make yourself feel enslaved. No one has this power over you. Only we can give our power away, no one can take it.

Bring your power back, don't allow others to push your boundaries, manipulate you, or hurt you. Choose to SEE the bigger picture, see the imbalances and the real, Authentic Being behind the imbalances and the masks, and feel the compassion, the empathy, and the non- judgment set in, instead. Know that crisis and imbalance are just showing up to help you and others to wake up, to see past duality and imbalance to Unity and to Love.

Next time, what will you choose to see?

Think of how many people you know, which most likely may include you, who have had the most horrific experiences and childhoods, having experienced every kind of physical, verbal and sexual abuse, and who, at some point in their journey, came to understand the piece we are speaking of, and chose to see the good, chose to see the Light and the Love? I, myself, had a childhood that involved all kinds of abuse at a very young age, most of us have, and I cannot help but smile when I see others who have suffered as much as myself, and more, and who have regained their light, and have gone on to give hope to others, to shine, to assist others with this piece and to bring Love and light into the world, and awaken people.

When I think of this I get a smile on my face, and think of how many have found themselves and are leading Sacred Lives of Service. One such person who always comes to mind when I think of this piece is Oprah. She suffered through terrible situations and has become a beacon of Hope and Choice in the world. "Are you living your best life?" she asks. Her whole series was about choice. *Are you doing your internal work?* This is the key to a life of Happiness. Everything is inside…. find It! Everything you are looking for is in You …YOU ARE THE ONE.

The teacher you long for *is* you

Take the time to know yourself and discover who you are; you are your biggest Teacher. It will blow your mind to find out how beautiful you are, how much Light you have, how much capacity for Love you have, and that it is eternal and endless. Oprah, to me, is a bridge to spirit; her life is a dedication to Service and to Spirit.

She has followed her Heart and has raised the vibration of the whole planet: She is the power of One.

Crisis is a time of evaluation, of introspection and opportunity and a choice point. What will you choose next time, to stay in separation and blame yourself and others, or will you choose Balance, Harmony, Love and Light?

> *"Our deepest fear is not that we are inadequate. Our deepest fear is that we are powerful beyond measure. It is our light, not our darkness, which frightens us most. We ask ourselves, 'Who am I to be brilliant, gorgeous, talented, and famous?' Actually, who are you not to be? You are a child of God. Your playing small does not serve the world. There is nothing enlightened about shrinking so that people won't feel insecure around you. We were born to make manifest the glory of God that is within us. It's not just in some of us; it's in all of us. And when we let our own light shine, we unconsciously give other people permission to do the same. As we are liberated from our own fear, our presence automatically liberates others."*
>
> *Marianne Williamson*

CHAPTER 5

SIGNS

I teach a meditation and intuition class I call "Becoming One." One day, when I was teaching in New York, the class began asking about the number 11.11.11, or a form thereof, and why this number was coming up so often recently on clocks, billboards, signs, and numerous other settings. I had just finished a session with someone on this same topic and I had previously taught a class on it, so I had a lot of information, some personal and some that had been posted on the Internet. To me, the information meant "wake up." It was a spiritual sign encoded within us, telling us to wake up to who we are, to Spirit within, a remembrance or trigger mechanism that was Universal in all. My friends Shawne and Cammie were in the class that day and suddenly, as I was speaking, Cammie yelled out, "Oh my gosh, look at the clock." The clock read 11:11.

And the clock had stopped.

We continued the class and the clock began to move again… eleven minutes later. We laughed and gave thanks to the Universe. As soon as class finished and we went downstairs, someone came into the center and said, "I have a question for anyone here. Why do I keep seeing the number 11:11? What does it mean?" We all burst out laughing again and explained what had just happened upstairs. We asked her to run upstairs and check the clocks in both studios. She did, and when she came back she said, "One clock is behind the other… by eleven minutes." So fun!

One day when I was meditating, I connected to my guides, two ascended masters, who spoke to me and relayed information to me as to the work I would be doing in the future. I was told I would be helping others to figure out who they are, and why they are here, and that I would assist people through their ascension process. On a more global level I would help bring in here, along with many others, the energy of Heaven on Earth. I was told that the next few years for me would be an intense time of remembering, of learning, and of tapping into other lifetimes and to the gifts and tools I had used in those lifetimes. I was told I would have many teachers, some within and some in my external world, and that I would be completing what would be like an accelerated graduate course. I was told I would have clairvoyance, clairsentience, clairaudience, and so on, as well as direct knowing. I was told I would become a medical intuitive, healer, and teacher.

The day I connected to the other side was a most amazing day in my life. I felt I had stumbled upon the biggest treasure on earth. I was sitting on a beach of gold. What made it even more powerful was that that beach is accessible to each and every one of us …that filled my heart with Love. I could not stop smiling, especially because all I kept thinking all day long and giggling about was, "Wow, we spend our whole life looking for happiness, love, and the secrets of life outside of ourselves. We journey far and wide and all the time what we are looking for is WITHIN! What a fabulous hiding place.

We spend our life looking for the key and the key is us!!!! "

All these messages were fabulous, and I cannot tell you how I felt…..so much Love…Peace….Grace. But then a few days later - practicality. *Am I going out of my mind? Is this real? I am a banker, not an intuitive. What the hell is that?*

So the messages kept coming, and I had only one request. I needed two things. One: proof, in this reality, that Spirit was real, with tangible evidence of its existence on this realm. And two: proof that the work I was being told I could do was in fact accurate, good, and would lead people Home.

The first thing I did was to go see a beautiful intuitive named Isabel, someone I came to understand later has been my sister through many lifetimes. I went down to Virginia, where she helped me by teaching me how to navigate through what I was seeing with my inner sight. After that trip I had the affirmation and confirmation I needed. We spent a week together and then she introduced a third person I did not know, whom we would do readings on separately . We would tune in intuitively and receive messages for this person seated before us, write them down on a piece of paper, and compare our answers. Amazingly they were always the same, and were also acknowledged as true by the person we were working on. We went in and scanned her body for past and current physical ailments as well as mental, emotional, and spiritual pieces, and those too were the same. It was the validation I needed on this plane that the work was real and that I was capable.

Spiritual breadcrumbs leading us Home

At the same time, I began to receive tangible proof of the existence of Spirit in the form of signs and messages. I will share some of the signs I received. My purpose in sharing them with you is that I hope they may also give you what they have given me—validation that Spirit is real, and that we are not alone.

I have received so many signs in my lifetime that I have come to believe the *only* thing real is Spirit, and that signs are the way Spirit weaves itself into our reality, like breadcrumbs leading us Home. Our world is not real, it is but an illusion put in place to help us evolve, a place for us to experience. Spirit, however, does very tangibly weave itself into the illusion. Every time I receive a sign I cannot help but smile and be grateful!

My dad and I had always had a special relationship, one that extended to his amazing ability with ESP. His ESP was so strong that he and a friend of his were going to go to Duke University to participate in a study on ESP. They never actually got there, but that is another story for another time. Here is our part of our story. My family would love to play charades, and often when my dad would stand up to play, I would say whatever it was he wrote on the piece of paper in his hand before he even got started. If he thought of me, or was sad, or in pain, I could feel him.

One day I was with my soon-to-be-husband, to whom I was slowly introducing my intuitive side, when suddenly I told him I was feeling my dad, and that he was sad, or trying to reach me; I even showed him the goose bumps on my arms indicating Spirit communication.

He said, "OK I will be open, Call your dad." I did, and the first thing my father said to me was, "Thank God you're home. Sorry I called you eight times, but I really needed to speak to you." I told him I was not home yet and had not received the phone messages, but instead I had received "the message."

Raindrops and messages keep falling

My father loved the song, "Raindrops Keep Falling on My Head," and every time I heard the song I knew he was sending a message. My husband, Joel, and I once left on a trip to Spain. Before we left, I had the premonition that my dad would pass while we were gone. My dad, who had been ill in the past, was healthy when we left, but I had gotten a sign from the birds that his time was near: Hundreds of blackbirds had graced my back lawn before I left. I tuned in, as I do, to see if I should travel anyway. I felt that I should go, as I was not to be with my dad when he passed, or so I thought.

We arrived in Spain, and a few days later we went to lunch in a place where there is a piano bar. As we walk in, the man behind the piano starts playing—you guessed it!—

"Raindrops Are Falling on My Head." Later we sat down to dinner at a different restaurant and the same song came on. The next day we sat down to lunch … and there it was again. This was in 2004, not a popular year for that song. I knew it was my father, trying to reach me, so I gave in and finally called home and my mom's friend answered. I asked if my dad was ill, and had he been ill for two days? She said yes, and that he was presently in the hospital. She told me he was well taken care of, and that I need not return home, but that they would keep me posted from then on.

Days passed, and as I sent my dad lots of Love and Light, I still felt it was his time to go Home. My dad had been raised by the Jesuits, and he always said they made priests and atheists; my dad was in the latter category, believing there was nothing after death. I had had my near-death experience by then, connecting to the other side, and as much as I tried to convey to him that this shell of a body we all possess is not who we are, that we live on past its existence, he was not able to believe. His fear was too big.

We will discuss this further in a minute, but I would like to digress to the subject of signs for a moment.

Joel, who was my husband at that point, had begun to ask me about signs, how they worked and how I received so many and he did not. I told him that maybe the signs are always there, but we are not conscious or aware or awake enough to see and feel them. So he decided he would try this sign thing. I told him this was the deal: First he needed to actively ask for a sign and then, the most important part –he had to be PRESENT i.e. aware, in the NOW moment, looking, seeing, and perceiving at all times, AWAKE. So Joel proceeded to ask for a sign from his father and mother, both of whom had passed. He was clear, he wanted to see their names, Sidney and Julia, in print somewhere before he arrived back in the US, and added the stipulation that Sidney could *not* be represented by Sydney, Australia.

A few days went by, and as we were walking down a beautiful, busy cobbled stone road in Spain, Joel asked me why his signs were taking so long. I asked him, "Have you been present and aware?" He answered, "Yes." I then asked, "Are you present and aware now?" And he responded, "Yes." So I said to him, "If so, then look around...." And sure enough, he looked around at a very large pharmacy next to him with its name in giant letters, from floor to ceiling: JULIA.

Later, we were on the plane going back to New York, and I had forgotten about the signs. As we were about to land in New York, Joel turned to me and said, "I guess I will not be getting a sign from my dad." One minute later we were watching the TV prompt in front of us, showing us a map and the plane's path into New York, and lo and behold, there is the name "Sidney" on the map of Canada. Did you ever know there is a Sidney somewhere in the northeast? We didn't.

Words uttered in more than one dimension

Back to my dad. During one of the evenings in Spain, I went to sleep and had a most vivid and real dream and was sure that my dad had passed. In the dream my dad had indeed passed and I was helping him cross to the other side. It was so Beautiful, so full of Love and light there. As my father approached me, he just radiated Love and Light, and I asked him "Daddy, are you happy?" (For so often he had said to me there is nothing after death) He said to me, "I have never been happier." He then asked, "But what are you doing here? You are not dead?" I said that I could not stay,, but that his friend Sergio would take care of him, and I said goodbye to both and came back and woke up in my bed.

The next morning I called home and asked if my dad had passed, as I was sure he had, and my mother said that he hadn't. It surprised me, since these vivid dreams in the past had usually reflected the reality on this plane.

My father passed three days later. On that day I asked for a sign. My heart was filled with sadness, with Love and with gratitude, and I asked that I receive a sign that would reflect how much my dad and I had loved each other, at a soul level, for there had been a great connection in this life but some of them had been out of balance too. So Joel and I left to walk the streets of Spain, and I found my sign. I could not stop crying. I wish I had taken a picture. Someday I will find this statue again. It was a life-size statue of a man holding his baby in his arms, and in big letters underneath the statue the name "NAVARRO," my dad and my last name.

After my dad was cremated, we spread his ashes

in the ocean, tied messages written to him on helium balloons, and let them go. The family was together for a few days, reminiscing and telling stories. During this time, several of the "girls" were in my mom's room, chatting, with a few of us on the bed and under the covers, including my mom, my Tia Helen, and my cousin Tara. I was saying to my mom that I had had such a vivid dream that dad has passed three days before he actually passed, and I told them the dream.

My mother's breath almost stopped. She choked up, and said, "Your dad slipped into unconsciousness three days before he passed, and the only words he uttered in his sleep during that time were, 'I have never been happier' and 'Can I have some tomato soup?' So the words he uttered to me in my dream were his last on this side, as well as the first words he uttered from the other side.

Another sign: When Joel and I met, I introduced him slowly to my intuitive side. While I do believe we should all be transparent and unmasked, I also ask for guidance when it comes to the pace and words with which it's best for me to reach someone, in order to assist in their journey, so I can be sure not to close them down, but to open them. So I did not bombard him with messages, but from time to time I would say, "I knew that was going to happen," or that I knew a certain person was going to call, or we were going to bump into them. So he said to me, "Why do you always tell me after the fact, why don't you tell me before? I need to hear it before, not after if it happens."

I think it was a few days or weeks later, on a weekend morning, when I was meditating in the hot tub outside our home. I had reached this amazing, beautiful place, feeling just so connected to everything, when I received this message: *You need to get out of the hot tub.*

Do I have to, really? I feel great right here, can't I receive the message here? I replied telepathically.

Here was my answer: *Because you haven't asked for a personal message in such a long time, but instead you have been relaying messages to so many out of Love and Service, we wish to give both of you a message today. For you, the message is just gratitude for your being who you are, thanking you for the courage it has taken to come out and do your work, and for the steps you have taken in your life that have brought you here today, and have brought you closer to us, and for that we are grateful.*

As for Joel, as he is journeying into Spirit and discovering himself from within; we want to give him a tangible

sign of Spirit in his reality. And for both of you, to under-
stand that your union is birthed and embraced with Light
and Spirit and so much Love and understanding, we pour
our Love, as One, into both of you and your journey.

The mysterious message

Then I was told to write a message down on a piece
of paper, to leave it inside the house, and to make sure
that when Joel arrived I was outside the house. This was
the message I was told to write: "Joel will arrive today
with a rose for you, red or white." That was it.

So I left the warmth and comfort of the hot tub,
wrote my message, and placed it in the house. I made
sure I was out of the house when Joel arrived. He got
out of the car and, sure enough, he had a rose in his
hand. I started to laugh and giggle. He looked at me
and asked, "What is so funny?" I said, "Go in the house
and look for a piece of paper on my desk that is behind
the picture of Alex [my brother] and read it." He came
out smiling; we hugged, and I said to him, "I guess what
they were talking about is that the rose was a white rose,
but on the edge of the rose was a pink or red border."

He laughed, "No you don't understand, you don't
understand. I stood in the flower shop with a white rose

in one hand and a red one in the other and asked myself which one I should bring you!"

That was the day I learned to deliver messages exactly as I get them, without filtering or altering, for, as I have come to learn through experience, it is better not to interpret, for you might then miss the real message.

When I was living in London, many years ago, I had to go in for a cone biopsy of my uterus and, to make a long story short, they nicked me in the process. Though I stayed in the hospital for several weeks at a time, they could not stop the bleeding. One night I was at home, though there was still a problem, and all of a sudden I found myself dying, crossing over. My life did flash in front of me; it was as if slides were being shown to me of different times during my life and then the Light… the amazing Light. All of a sudden I was immersed in Light and I *was* Light. I could see 360 degrees around, in all directions, all around the LOVE. The immense love! The feeling was amazing, and constant, a feeling that I could only maintain very fleetingly in life, and only during the most special moments, such as when I laid eyes on my children for the first time, that kind of feeling of Love. But this did not go away. I was welcomed and told I was Home. I took that in, and then said, "I am not ready. I have not finished my work. My children! I have to go back, so much unfinished."

I was told that I could go back, but that I did not have to, that even during this life I had lived out of service and choice, that I did not even need to be here, and that if I chose to go back it would be hard and difficult. I chose to return anyway, and instantly found myself back in my bed. Oh how horrible, the sense of being in body! Immediately I felt as if heavy bricks had been placed on my chest, with high anxiety, extreme heaviness, and difficulty breathing. An instant later, I was back in the light and given the choice again.

This happened three times, and three times I chose to come back. The third return stuck. The next day I called my internist, not the gynecologist, and explained the situation. He had me see another doctor the same day, who found a large dark black mark in my uterus. The two doctors and I decided it was time for me to fly to the US to get more answers there. I spoke to my doctor in the US and he said he was ready to see me and take my case on. We calculated when I would be menstruating and decided to postpone the trip for a few weeks.

During those weeks I felt pretty tired and ill, but a new symptom had appeared, apart from the tiredness and the bleeding, and this was nausea. My husband at the time had seen this before, as we already had three beautiful boys together, and he innocently asked, "Av, could you be pregnant?" And I, of course, responded, "And when do you suppose that could have happened?" I had been so sick, to be honest, I could not remember the last time we had had sex. But the nausea persevered, so I did a pregnancy test. In the past I had had very romantic ways of telling my husband I was pregnant. The first time we had both just gotten home from the office and I asked him to check out our dinner in the oven. He came back and said "Are we are having a roll for dinner?" "No," I said, "What else do you think it might mean?" He finally got it..."Bun in the oven."

During the second pregnancy I was in the shower as he returned home and came into the bathroom to chat. We lived in a small two-bedroom apartment in the city and had just finished decorating the second bedroom as a study, spending very little money. I then proceeded to tell him that I thought the study turned out all wrong, that especially the color of the walls was wrong and that maybe it shouldn't be a study at all. He asked me if I was feeling OK, since the day before I had been so happy with the way it had turned out. Finally I just said we plainly picked the wrong color for the walls, they definitely needed to be pink or blue. Silence ensued and then he said "A baby?"

The next time it was "The rabbit died," which was the old fashioned way of saying a woman was pregnant, having to do with the sort of pregnancy test we all unfortunately used at the time, and I greeted him with a miniature stuffed bunny rabbit lying on a bed of cotton balls holding a miniature flower on its chest. The time after that I greeted him at the door holding a door handle placed strategically on my body as if I were a door, with a sign pointing up…knocked up.

A baby's brave choice

This time was different. I had just died and come back and was still wondering how I would take care of myself, my three children, and the possibility of a newborn baby. I must say I just starting wailing…not so romantic! However; in retrospect I see that it was one of the most special moments of my life. Days later the pregnancy was confirmed, and I was well into my third month. However, the doctor wanted to end the pregnancy out of concern for my health, specifically the black spot on the uterus, where I was still bleeding. I told him that I had not come back from the light with this baby only to end its life, and if the baby was going, then we were both going together.

My beautiful baby girl was born months later; the black mark healed magically as the pregnancy progressed and the bleeding completely stopped. Years later, I went to see an intuitive like myself and despite not revealing anything about myself, she said to me, "You know both you and your daughter aren't really supposed to be here; she chose to come back with you. She, too, was done with reincarnating. In her last life she was a renowned healer whom people traveled from far away to see, and her first healing in this lifetime was in utero. And it was you."

The answer received before it was sent

The signs and synchronicities never end when we are expecting them. And they so often reach us through the animal kingdoms.

The morning after I had the luminous experience of Oneness with my son, I got up and ready to teach my intuition and meditation class in New York. As I opened the garage I noticed a white animal on my lawn, and stopped the car to get out to see. As I did so, I swear, the leaves and the lawn were infused with this incredible golden light, and I knew a potent message had been coming through for days. I looked at the garden to see a white animal walking toward me. It was a giant white rat who came to me and stopped right at my feet, looking up to me.

I knew it carried a message for me, so I stared into its eyes for a while until it turned around, left my garden, and disappeared. After teaching, I went home and looked on the Internet to find out what this animal was trying to tell me. There were a lot of references to seeing a rat, including messages about death, plague, disease, and so on, but nothing about a white rat. I found that they were not usually found in nature and, being nocturnal, were hardly ever seen during the day. I finally hit upon a site that included a comment from a woman in California who was responding to the following posted question: "I was approached by a white rat at a gas station. Does anyone know what that might mean?" The woman answered, "The white rat represents Spirit, Light, blessings coming to you. And since you are at a gas station, it means you need to fill your life up more with things of Love and Spirit." I noted her name and email and called her to thank her for the message.

Soon after, I was taking my daily bath, which I never interrupt, since it is my quiet sanctuary time. The phone rang, and I got the clear message, "Go answer the phone; it is the woman in California." So I wrapped a towel around me, picked up the phone, and sure enough it was the woman from California. Her name was Lucia. As I related how grateful I was that she had posted the message about the rat, she laughed!!! "I haven't posted it yet. How did you get to it?" I said, "I just found it on the Internet...how funny is that! You haven't posted it, yet I found it."

It seemed Spirit was having fun and playing. I asked her what she did for a living. She said she was a healer and an intuitive, helping people to figure out who they are and why they are here. It was now my turn to laugh, as I told her I do the same! She told me it was time for her to come out of her cocoon, and that she had been guided to stop her bodywork, expand her healing practice and branch out to the Internet. Well, I told her the universe wanted her to know that her new approach is working and that it has already reached me. I told her about my experience with the white rat and she said she thought it was a message from Spirit and the angels saying they are with you, your home, and your work of bringing it to others.

It is such a beautiful way that spirit weaves its way into our reality.

Cherie dies three times

Another Sign: My friend Cherie and I have journeyed together in this lifetime and beyond. I met Cherie years ago, when she came for a session and then followed up by coming to my evening meditation and healing classes. As much fun as they were, I found that after the evening classes I became too tired, and had to give them up. I had learned my lesson all too well by then, one that still circulates my periphery so often, that what we do to please others, without first taking care of ourselves, serves no one.

Since Cherie worked during the day and could not make my day classes, we ended up seeing each other less often, and mostly at holiday parties., One Monday morning I received a message from within that I was to clear my upcoming schedule of sessions on Friday, so I did not book anything, figuring I needed a break and my garden needed tending. Soon I received a call from Cher that she needed to see me on Friday, and I got the message that I was to see her. It was important, and of course my calendar was open, for I thought I was to have the afternoon off.

So Cher showed up at my door, and as soon as I saw her I felt that she was fading, she is losing her life force, and quickly. She still looked healthy and young outwardly; my husband was present but could not see what I saw.

I brought Cherie into my office, and we began our session as messages meant for her from Spirit quickly began to flow. They were all about choices, about finding our compass, and realizing that the only person who knows what is right for us, is us, and no one else, about how there is no "good" or "bad" once we reach a certain point in the spiritual journey. It was about choices, her choices, though I did tell her that if it were I, I would be going to the hospital as soon as I could, for I saw her body was under terrible stress and needed assistance. I also told her she needed to follow what she felt was right from now on, and not to listen to me or anyone except herself, and do what felt right for her.

We did some healing, getting her a little stronger, and I told her to rest on my healing bed for as long as she needed, while I would be close by in the garden.

Outside, my husband asked why there was still a car in the driveway, and I explained to him that Cher was not doing well, and was resting, but that I felt she was struggling physically and needed to go to the hospital soon. Cher came out about an hour later, looking and feeling much better. So, even though I had told her that I would be going to the hospital directly from my session if I were Cherie, I did not know when and if she would choose to go, and whatever she chose I knew would be perfect and in Divine Order.

Crossing Over with Cherie

The next day I heard that Cher had waited a day, then gone to the hospital, and as soon as she arrived at the hospital all her organs began to shut down, one by one, as she fell into a coma. After this incident I checked on her in meditation every day. During the time she was in her coma she died three times. I find the number interesting, as that was the same number of times I went into to the light. One morning, as I was checking on her and sending her healing Light and Love, we began to chat telepathically, and she told me she remembered her last session with me on earth, when we discussed choices and that she understood now, on so many levels, what this meant, and what the choice in front of her was: Am I to stay on the earth or am I to cross over?

Cher said she understood the earth choice, but was having a problem understanding the second choice. She asked, "What did crossing over mean, and how did it feel?" So I asked her "Do you want to go see? So you can make a choice?" She said, "Yes, but can you come with me?" I answered 'Yes, I can come with you."

And we crossed over together. The next day, when I went in to check her field, I saw that her body was being filled with Light, and knew a miracle was underfoot; her body was being restored to health and she had chosen to stay on earth. I was so happy, selfishly, to have her here in the physical, and I am always moved to tears when I see this, for it is no easy choice. It is incredibly painful and hard to move down into density from the Light, a choice that is always made out of Love and Service. It takes so much courage, and I am always so incredibly touched by the love that comes with it.

I had been keeping my meditation group abreast of Cher, her progress, her impending decision whether to stay or go, and how we had crossed over together in order to help her decide. and that I was now seeing her body full of light and felt she was returning to life.

Cher miraculously began to get better, her organs one by one began to come back, and they started calling her the Miracle Girl. Everything came back except her heart. She had to be given an artificial heart, with a battery-operated bionic pump, to keep her alive, but even that, to the astonishment of her doctors, may soon be removed, as they believe her heart is healing.

A vision of Whitney working in Spirit

Every time Cherie goes to the doctors, they say to her, "We do not know how you are sitting in front of us, and even if your body came back we do not know how you are not brain dead." I cannot tell you how many people prayed for Cher. Every time I went in to do healing work on her, which was every morning for months, I would see in my meditation my dear friend Whitney, also working on Cher, so it was no wonder that when Cher came out of her coma, one of the first things she asked was, "Where is Whitney?" She thought she had been physically with Whitney the whole time, but Cher was in New York, while Whitney was in South Africa.

Cher couldn't wait to see Whitney and me. In particular, she wanted to share her experience with me. She said she saw me as all light, but she knew it was me. She said my light was in her, for we were together as One the whole time. She remembers speaking telepathically to me and our crossing over together It was exhilarating to me that she remembered the experience, as so often people do not. I share only what Cher has shared with the world and I have kept the rest of our sessions and conversations as private, as I would with anyone. We are blessed that she is still with us and I am very grateful for that. She is another Angelic presence here, spirit walking, what better sign than that!

A call to go Home

A few months ago, I got the call to go to France. It was not the ideal time to go, for many reasons, but the pull was so strong, and the message I received was that I needed to go on my own, not with a specific group. The message indicated I could piggyback on an existing tour, but that I should be journeying mostly by myself and shouldn't follow any preset schedule. The journey took me to various places in France, but most of my trip was in the Rennes les Château area. The message I received, through meditation and through others, was that I was going "Home." A few days after I arrived in Rennes, I had an open day and I got the message to spend some time at a restaurant in Rennes owned by two lovely people named Toby and Gerda. As I was sitting there, talking to Gerda, whom I felt I had known forever, with whom I felt an instant connection, I got the message that I should meditate at the Magdalene Tower. So off I went. I meditated first at the smaller tower with the glass conservatory, and then proceeded to the actual tower. I was there alone, and in a corner of the tower, began playing my singing bowl, in order to begin my meditation.

Unbeknownst to me, a French woman named Benedictine, who lived four hours away, had been given the message to be there on that day and at that time in order to meet with an American woman who was a healer, intuitive, and that she and this woman would be doing some work together. She had had four readings by four different people, four months earlier, and they had all told her the same thing.

On the very same date we met, she saw another intuitive who gave her the same message. She, like me, heard the call and followed Spirit. But on that given day, I was not there when she reached the tower, and her heart sank. She took a small stroll and came back five minutes later. This time, when she reached the bottom of the tower and started ascending the stairs, she heard the sound of a singing bowl, and her heart fluttered as she sensed that something magical was happening.

When she reached the top I had my eyes closed, but I sensed her presence and opened them. As soon as I saw her I felt recognition, and she immediately asked: "Are you American? Are you a healer?" and I answered" Yes," She began to cry. It was a most powerful time together, so much Love. We did the work we needed to do, journeyed through the building next to the tower, sharing, connecting, laughing, and marveling at Spirit. Next we decided to go back to Gerda's place and have a bite to eat.

We arrived and Gerda came to say Hi. I introduced Benedictine and shared our story. Gerda said to me, "You know you are Home." I said "Yes, that's the message I received before leaving the US." Gerda then brought out the most beautiful book, bound in leather with a fleur de lis on the cover, asking me and Benedictine to sign it. Three times I asked if she was certain about that, as it was an extraordinary book. It was an illuminated manuscript made by Toby, her husband, with the most beautiful paintings. I recognized the names of some of those who had signed it, and somehow I felt, "Me? Are you sure?" And she said, "Yes you are family." I was honored. Benedictine and I were happy to have spent this beautiful time together. We exchanged our contact information on small pieces of scrap paper, having nothing else at hand, and said our goodbyes, knowing we would be connected forever.

That evening I went to dinner with my friend Gloria, a dear friend and someone who made this trip possible and who I am blessed to have in my life. Gloria invited her friend Nancy, and Nancy and I sat next to each other. When Nancy asked me, "How was your day?" I said to her, "I had the most amazing day," and I told her about meeting this beautiful woman at the Magdalene tower, who had been told by no fewer than five people to be there so we could meet. Nancy started to laugh, and said, "You are the American woman?" I answered, "Yes, how did you know?" She said, "Because I did a reading for her this morning, and I too got the message that she was to go there and meet with the American woman."

We laughed. When I returned home I looked for the scrap piece of paper with Benedictine's information on it, and of course I could not find it. She, too, must have lost mine, as she has not been in touch, either. However, I do have Nancy trying to track her down and Benedictine, if you read this, contact me. I would love to be in touch again. In the meantime, I know I am not in charge of these things and am blessed that at least we had that time together.

Bendable laws, bendable spoons

We are not separate; we are One, and as such we are all human, but are all also Divine, and it is this Divinity that Unites us as One.

When I am in the field of knowing this, it just all feels like Love, unimaginable Love, unconditional Love. We were all created equal and in the image of God. Everything that has ever existed is and always will be Divine, stemming from our Creator. There is no separation from Source, separation is but an illusion

We just need to Remember.

A few weeks before I left for my trip to France, I began receiving messages in meditation, in my practice, and from friends, that the time for miracles and for the bigger gifts is upon us, and as we move into the Unified Field, we would see exceptions to the laws of nature, as we know them. Spontaneous healings would begin to happen, and things that defy the laws of gravity would happen. Nobody had to make me a believer. I had seen enough people in my practice get better; I had gotten better myself many a time.

I continued receiving messages saying that phenomena like levitation and spoon-bending would be part and parcel of these changes, and that we should begin to start playing with these concepts. I then asked myself and spirit what purpose there could possibly be for spoon bending and levitation? How does that assist us in becoming One, in remembering who we are? So I began my dialogue with Spirit. I was told that they would help by presenting tangible physical evidence of Spirit and of the existence of the Unified Field, of Unity, and of Love. I said, "Great, but is this an exclusive club, only for the few, or is it for everyone? And is everyone capable of these things and can everyone access this Field?" Would these abilities be a side effect of being on your spiritual path that everyone would have access to? For I really wasn't interested if it was to be only accessible to some -- we have already created that world.

The world I am much more interested in is the New World, where we create everything in Union for the good of all. The answer was of course, *Yes*, and that we access these abilities from Within and by doing the "Work," much of which I have discussed in this book.

The point being that if people were to see these things that defy reality as we know it, their inner work of figuring out who they really are and why they are here would accelerate. So I decided that if it served all and anyone, and I mean that anyone could do it, I would try it.

So I decided I would try it out by bending a spoon. I took a spoon I could not normally bend, meditated with it in my hands, thereby connecting to it, using my heart with Love and Presence. I sent Love and imagined the spoon and I vibrating faster. Soon the spoon became warm and I was able to bend it in a corkscrew fashion, twice around itself. Why is this a sign? To me it is physical manifestation of how *all* of our interior work is done, of how healing happens, of how our thoughts and energy create reality, of how we manifest everything.

This was not about bending the spoon. When I go in to bend the spoon, I am not thinking "Bend the spoon," I am connecting to the place where the spoon and I are the same, where we are One and where all the Love is. Inherently, everyone can do this. It can be done if you can be still long enough to connect to yourself first, to your inner voice, to Love, to your Heart, and then, from that place, connect to everyone and everything.

For it is Love that binds all.

CHAPTER 6

LOVE LOVE LOVE

Love is all there is. I went through a difficult time in my life when my body was struggling and riddled with pain. I had a physical condition, confirmed by my doctors, which stripped the lining of the inside of my bladder, causing excruciating pain, but for which there was no cure, and painkillers were not an option. This condition had been with me for almost two months, though I had consulted all form of doctors, healers, and connected to my own healing modalities, with absolutely no relief. Life was becoming unbearable. Then one of my children, without any rhyme or reason, sat on my bed and made a loud sound, directed at the lower part of my body, and in a few minutes the pain that had been with me for months left me. I asked him "Why did you do that?" He answered, "I just knew what I had to do to make you better."

The miracle of Healing, Remembrance, and Love!

Love is all there is, Love is all there is, Love is all there is.

The Beatles got it right, all you need is Love, Love, Love is all you need. Nothing else matters. All we need to do is to Remember this, and to Remember this we just need to Remember who we are. This is our inward journey Home to becoming One. And what are the gates and portals to get there?

Here they are.

Acceptance: of everything, exactly as it is, no resistance, knowing that things are perfect just the way they are.

Clarity: to know when to speak, when to place a boundary, when to stay silent and just witness, or when to go in and add our own energy and wisdom to any situation.

Non-judgment: realizing that there is no right or wrong, just differences, that everyone and everything is Divine and is of equal value, and that every single path is valid.

Love thy neighbor as thyself: There is only One of

Us here, and you are part of each and every one, so treat everyone the way you would like to be treated yourself.

Gratitude: Be grateful for everything in your life, even the things you deem as "bad" or "uncomfortable," as they, too, will take you Home.

Forgiveness: of yourself and others.

Sacred Life, Sacred Being: See the sacred in everything, loving it just the way it is. **Be the change in the world by changing the way you see the world.** Allow love to permeate all you are doing, and you will live in a state of "Being," a state of Love instead of a state of "doing."

Authenticity: Be yourself, and eventually all you will Be is Love and Service.

Be Present: Live in the Now; that's all that is real; it is where the magic lives.

Co-Create: Spend time manifesting the world you wish to be in; you are the One and you are the One you have been waiting for; create the change you want to see in the world by changing you, one person at a time from the inside out. The more you know, the less you know.

Reality: The idea of right and wrong is only based

on where you are sitting, the perception and the perspective you have. Give it up, for as you change and evolve, so will your reality.

Love: Love everyone and everything, especially your enemies.

Thoughts create reality: What are you thinking? What are you creating? Be part of something greater than yourself: Find that piece of you that is part of the Whole, part of the Creator, part of God, and Be that.

Filling our world with the unseen

Follow the above, and Co-Create from Oneness, and this will be Heaven on Earth. Find it here, right here, right Now. Allow yourself to shine, to dream big. I love the Marianne Williamson statement that our deepest fear is not that we are inadequate, but that we are powerful beyond measure.

At some point in our journey, everything shifts from what we have been taught by our peers, our teachers, our parents, our community, to our Teacher within, and everything changes, from a linear outer focus to an inner Experience. We begin to shift inside, suddenly finding insight we did not have before, and we see with different Eyes.

The next step takes a lot of courage, and that is **Surrender.** We have to give it all up, it is as if everything we have ever been taught to be true and everything we had held onto so tightly have to be let go of. **Then, and only then, when we have become liberated from everything of this world, can the unseen fill our world.** The unseen is not linear and cannot be described, as there are no words for it. It is not of this world. It can only be Experienced. The closest way of describing it is to say that we experience Grace. After this transformation occurs, which to others is unseen, then it really doesn't matter what we do, going forward, or how we do it. For whatever we do will be Sacred, it will be a Life in Service to God, and whatever we Create and do will be for the good of all.

There will have been an internal shift as we live more in the Present, as we are of Service. It will be more about holding this beautiful energy that resides within us and magnifying it into the world. It is about Being in this world but not of it. All that we had been taught to see as good or bad disappears, all the struggle about who is right and who is wrong disappears, when we invite this Omnipresence in.

Eventually, if we are truly looking with earnest sincerity and humility, the inward path, the path to God, becomes available to us. It is available to all, regardless of gender, race, sexual preference, or location. It is universal to mankind. No matter what external path you have followed up until now, Atheist, Christian, Jewish, Muslim, at some point in your journey of self-discovery everything points Home, and Home is inside of You.

We go from a path of outward study to actively connecting with Oneself, with One's Divinity. Eventually, if one has the courage and strength to do so, to Remember, we become One with God. We become the vessel, the vehicle, and the container for God and God's Work. Once we hit this place that can only be "Experienced," not really explained, and only reached through reflection, we come out of this experience having become the vessel of Light, and the only thing that matters after this, is leading a Sacred Life.

Why are we still choosing separation?

When One experiences Unity, Oneness, God, and Creation, Everything, it can feel as though we come with a new perspective to See all the places on this planet where there is still separation, to wonder, *Why are people still choosing this?* People are continuously separated by race, gender, sexual preference, religion, country, politics, money and power. In St. Teresa of Avila's *The Interior Castle*, she says, "The aim of a human life is Union with God; it is the transformation of our being and its divinization."

In the Christian Church, sainthood is bestowed upon those who are thought to have become One with God while still on earth. St. Teresa's message seems to be that such a state is available to all:

"What ultimately matters is not our ideas, or our experiences or our denying this or doing that, what 'matters' is not a method of prayer or a peculiar way of life; the all-important thing, the unique and ultimate end of man is sanctity, union with God, transformation in God, divinization of our full being."

I began all this by suggesting that you take from this book whatever works for you, and discard the rest. I also said that, though Spiritual truths are simple, the journey is difficult and takes a lot of courage. Why? Because I think, though people hear such statements as, "You are the key to what you are looking for," and "The kingdom of Heaven is within," with the idea that all you need to do is to go into quiet inner reflection or meditation and you will find Fulfillment, Love, Lightness of Being, Clarity or Wisdom, they don't believe it could be that simple. So they get sidetracked, going on with their daily lives, not going *in*, staying in the illusion, and remaining in the world of separation from God, from Source and from Love.

But these statements are true.

Everything you have always wanted, you possess inside you. You just need to sit still, Experience and Remember.

Please choose, choose to be Present, choose to connect to yourself and your Divinity: Choose Love. Please just try it; what do you have to lose? I cannot tell you how many people say to me "Yes, I will do it." Then they meditate for only a day or two before they give up.

If you are being offered the Holy Grail, why would you not take it? If you don't go within, you go without.

Is this the place that needs my Authenticity?

So start seeing the places in your world where people are discriminated against, shunned for things like their religion, gender, sexual preference, race, nationality, where separation is prevalent and used to control, to keep out, to uphold a sense of "We are better than them," or "We must preserve our way, in order to survive." This way of thinking rejects people for things they cannot change. See the places where you do not accept people because of their religious beliefs or where we do not let people participate or become leaders because of their gender or sexual preference. And start asking yourself *Is this a place where I can make a better world? Is this a place where we can accept each other and our Sacred differences and know we are all One, deserving to be part of the Whole, rather than being excluded from it?*

So go in Peace. Find your Joy, find your Passion, have fun, dance and sing, paint and create, and don't be so serious, find the laughter and the connection and the Lightness of Being. But, most important, find You and Love You, no matter what you have done or not done, for when you love yourself, you are Love, YOU ARE THE ONE.

Remember that what you send out eventually comes right back, so take that Love and send it to others unconditionally, learn to Love all. Especially Love your enemies, Love your shadow, and Love the dark, for how will we transform the world if we send more hatred to the hated? Instead, send love to those most in need. This is the only way to shed light in the dark and illuminate our way Home.

Bring in unconditional Love, be a part of something greater than yourself, and live a Sacred Life. Walk the walk and talk the talk, putting into practice the teachings, bringing the teachings to life.

In the end it is about being in this world but not of it. It is about being here and connected to Spirit, the unseen. That means finding your Joy, your Balance, your Love, and being Happy. And how do we do that? By reaching a State of Being where we understand that everything and anything that happens here is Divine and has purpose. By connecting to this greater Being within ourselves, we become part of something greater than ourselves and we begin to live the teachings, we begin to Experience the teachings. We start walking the walk and talking the talk. It is as if nothing changes and everything changes at once. It is our perspective that changes, and we start to Experience the Love of our Creator and we start seeing with the Eyes of our Creator. When this happens, we can't help but see through the imbalances to the Authentic being behind the masks and start living and Experiencing Unconditional Love. We come into Sacred Union with ourselves, with everyone, and everything, and with our Creator.

You are the key to the Sacred

The key to everything you are looking for in your life is YOU! Go within and find LOVE, LIGHT, CON-NECTION, UNITY, ABUNDANCE, JOY, LIGHT-NESS OF BEING, LAUGHTER, BLISS, HEALTH, BEAUTY, BALANCE, PEACE, FREEDOM AND FUL-FILLMENT. Do the WORK; it is the work of your life. It is why you are here. Find the Sacred in you and your life will become Sacred. Find Fulfillment in you first, and it will become manifest in your environment. Your thoughts create your reality, so what are you thinking and feeling? That will become your reality.

It is your choice as to how you think and feel about everything in your life. Will you choose fear and worry, or will you choose LOVE and LIGHT? Send LOVE to everything, especially your enemies, for if you are so full of light and they really need the light, why would you send them darkness? Hatred? Anger? Send them LOVE.

What comes around goes around, and guess what -- if we are all just One, then in this fast-paced world, where manifestations are coming faster and faster, it will only be a matter of minutes for your own thoughts to reach you. So if you send Love, then Love is what you will receive.

Stay in the Present moment, it is all that is real. It is the magic zone of creativity, where dreams become reality. Breathe and get out of your own way, and allow the greater You to grow within you and guide you. Find your inner voice, connect to your magical inner child, and look at the world through Her eyes. Don't take life so seriously. After all, if you know that everything is Divine and happening for a Divine reason, then why take things so seriously? Lose the drama and the victim roles, they don't help.

Empower yourself, and remove the masks by being your Authentic, vibrant, Beautiful piece. Be You. We all come into this world different, only to try to fit in and be the same! Find the original beauty of who You are. Find your puzzle piece and be It. When you see someone who has discovered who they are, their puzzle piece, you'll see that they are Vibrant and Beautiful. You, too, are that way, but don't try to be like them. The only way you can shine like them, is to be YOU. YOU ARE THE ONE.

So please, please, please take a minute each day to connect with yourself. You are what you have been waiting for; You are your biggest teacher. Everything lies within. Please, please GO WITHIN SO YOU DON'T GO WITHOUT. Connect to the Divine Spark within and become One with IT. Awaken the Divinity in You; connect to who You truly are. You always had IT, always will have It, It was always inside of You. Just REMEM-BER, you never separated from IT.

Ask for what you need, spend time giving thanks, and be grateful for what is in your life NOW. Focus on what you have now, not on what you don't have. Find the Beauty in your life by connecting to your Heart, as from this place you will find the Sacredness and the Peace you long for. Manifest what you want to feel in the future *Now*, and ask that it be available to you and to all. And if you are manifesting from your heart, it will come from the Unified Field in your heart, so anything you manifest will serve all and will not hurt anyone. It will serve everyone's highest good.

What you place your attention and intention on is what will manifest, so think positively. No matter how difficult the day, find a minute to say hello to the sun, say hello to the sunset, to the moon, to the earth and its creatures, and connect to Nature. Nature never came away from the Unified Grid. It can show you the way home. Find YOUR path, for it will lead you Home.

Yes, go in Peace. Know that you are not alone. Know

this: YOU ARE THE ONE, for you are part of the One-ness. Go within and connect to you where you are One and find your Compass, find your Breath, find your Passion, find your Joy, find your Laughter, find your Voice, find your Lightness of Being, find your Captain, find your Freedom, find You and find THE ONE.

Be of Service. Be a part of something greater than yourself. Just BE. And to get there:

LOVE is all you need, LOVE is all you need, LOVE is all you need, all you need is LOVE. LOVE........ LOVE............ that is all there is.

ABOUT THE AUTHOR

Writer Avis Baum is also a painter, teacher, and intuitive whose practice is designed to assist people in going within in order to discover who they are and why they are here. Born in Cuba, she grew up in Lima, Peru, and in the United States, and has lived in London as well as the US. After graduating from Smith College, she attained the distinction of becoming the youngest vice-president of the Bank of Boston, New York, later retiring to raise her children. During that period she had the series of near-death experiences she writes about in *You Are the One*, dying and returning three times, powerful events that clarified and intensified her intuitive gifts. The author lives and conducts her sessions in Fairfield County, Connecticut. Her website is AvisBaum.com.